BUDGET CONTROL
AND COST BEHAVIOR

ANDREW C. STEDRY

PRENTICE - HALL, INC.

Englewood Cliffs, N. J.

First printing .... *June, 1960*
Second printing .... *April, 1961*
Third printing ...... *December, 1961*

Foreword

This volume is one of five doctoral dissertations selected for publication in the first annual Doctoral Dissertation Competition sponsored by the Program in Economic Development and Administration of The Ford Foundation. The winning dissertations were completed during the academic year 1958-59 by doctoral candidates in business administration and doctoral candidates in the social sciences and other fields relevant to the study of problems of business.

The dissertation competition is intended to generalize standards of excellence in research on business by graduate students. It should give widespread professional recognition to persons recently awarded doctorates in business whose dissertation research is especially distinguished by its analytical content and strong roots in underlying disciplines. It is also intended to give recognition to a select number of persons outside business schools who in their doctoral dissertations pursued with distinction interests relevant to business.

The dissertations selected include, in addition to Dr. Stedry's monograph:

> *Computer Models of the Shoe, Leather, Hide Sequence*
> > Kalman J. Cohen
> > Graduate School of Industrial Administration
> > Carnegie Institute of Technology

> *Polya Type Distributions in Renewal Theory, with an Application to an Inventory Problem*
> > Frank Proschan
> > Department of Statistics
> > Stanford University

> *The Structure of a Retail Market and the Market Behavior of Retail Units*
> > Bob R. Holdren
> > Department of Economics
> > Yale University

> *Some Personality Determinants of the Effects of Participation*
> > Victor H. Vroom
> > Department of Psychology
> > University of Michigan

The many high-quality dissertations submitted were judged by the most exacting professional standards. Specific criteria included:

a. Importance of the problem and originality of approach;
b. Use of the most appropriate and powerful tools of analysis;
c. Clear relation to the relevant theoretical framework or a contribution to theory;
d. Direct relevance to the practice of business or management;
e. Clarity and effectiveness of presentation.

An examination of all five volumes in this series will reveal that four of the five make considerable use of mathematical and statistical tools. This reflects the increasing importance of modern quantitative methods in the study of business. On the other hand, the use of quantitative techniques should certainly not be considered a *sine qua non* of rigorous research in business. It is hoped that in future years it will be possible to select for publication a greater number of nonmathematical dissertations of the highest quality.

On behalf of The Ford Foundation, I wish to express my sincere appreciation to the Editorial Committee for its painstaking effort in selecting the winning dissertations. The scholars who served as members of the Committee for the first year's competition were Robert Ferber, Research Professor of Economics, University of Illinois; Sherman J. Maisel, Professor of Business Administration, University of California (Berkeley); and William Foote Whyte, Professor, New York State School of Industrial and Labor Relations, Cornell University.

The work of the Editorial Committee was materially aided by a group of six readers, who spent hundreds of hours in conscientious examination of the dissertations submitted. The Foundation and the Committee wish to thank Professors Austin C. Hoggatt and Julius Margolis of the University of California (Berkeley), Henry A. Landsberger and Seymour Smidt of Cornell University, and Vernon K. Zimmerman and Thomas A. Yancey of the University of Illinois for their service as readers in the first year of the competition.

Finally, my colleagues and I wish to acknowledge the substantial contribution of Prentice-Hall, Inc., to the publication and distribution of the selected dissertations.

THOMAS H. CARROLL
VICE PRESIDENT
THE FORD FOUNDATION

New York, New York
January, 1960

Preface

This study constitutes an attempt to bring to bear on a particular management problem — the problem of budgetary control — knowledge which is drawn from five disciplines: economics, psychology, organization theory, mathematics, and accounting.

It is difficult in a document of limited size to provide in every instance a comparison of the opposing or reinforcing views of the main bodies of theory in each of the disciplines. Furthermore, as is well known, each discipline has its own peculiar manner of expression. Thus, if it would appear at various points in this document that some lack of consistency in terminology is present, it should be understood that comparisons must often be drawn with terminology that is alien to one discipline or another.

The aim of this study is to explore various approaches to the problem of budget control, using tools supplied by the various disciplines where it is felt they are applicable. It might be said that the approach was thus "problem-oriented" rather than "tool-oriented." The three approaches that will be presented are (1) a mathematical systems model of individual behavior in a goal- or budget-striving situation, (2) an empirical investigation of the performance of individuals under varying budget conditions, and (3) the linear programming formulation which attempts to deal with some of the planning and coordinating aspects of budgeting. The means used for this attempt to at least provide a step in the direction of a scientific basis for budget control are sufficiently diverse in method that their approach to the same end is frequently not obvious. However, it would seem most unwise to attempt to solidify, at this stage of the development, any monistic line of inquiry into a subject which, albeit so old in the annals of history, is young in the annals of science.

ACKNOWLEDGMENTS

The work carried on in the thesis was in part supported by the Office of Naval Research to which I owe my thanks. Parts of the dissertation appear in more or less complete form as Office of Naval Research memoranda numbers 60, 61, and 63[1]. To the administrator of the proj-

—————
[1]References (75), (76), (77) of this thesis.

ect, Professor Peter R. Winters, and the director, Professor G. L. Bach, Dean of the Graduate School of Industrial Administration, Carnegie Institute of Technology, go my thanks for their aid in procuring the necessary funds for carrying out the empirical investigation.

I owe my thanks to the Graduate School of Industrial Administration in whose name fellowships were granted for the years 1957-59, during which time the research reported in this paper took place.

It would be virtually an impossible task to credit all of the people who have contributed to my academic background, and thus to the pursuit of the degree for which this paper is presented. I will, however, attempt to mention those who were most inspiring and helpful.

I have benefited greatly in the past from association with Professor Franco Modigliani whose lectures comprised the major part of my formal instruction in economic theory and with whose aid I have been able to publish my first journal article.[2] The idea upon which Chapter 2 is based was discussed with Professor Herbert A. Simon two years ago, and from this discussion, with Professor Simon's encouragement, the relationships between budgets, aspirations, and performance became the nucleus of the document.

The knowledge of psychology necessary to carry out this study was obtained with the aid of Professors Harold J. Leavitt, Walter Reitman, and Richard Willis, who directed me toward appropriate works in the field and discussed with me the plans for the empirical research to be reported.

I am deeply indebted to my committee, Professors William W. Cooper, Merton H. Miller, Richard M. Cyert, and Harold Leavitt for their full cooperation during the progress of the work. Their criticisms were constructive and helpful.

The experiment was performed with the aid of my colleague, Mr. Charles P. Bonini and Messrs. James Lemon, and Richard Young, students in the Graduate School of Industrial Administration.

I am indebted to Miss Sandra Kinney who typed the majority of the document, who faithfully devoted every night, and weekends as well for several weeks, in order to ensure the timely presentation of the document. Mrs. Joan Anderson came to my rescue at the eleventh hour when it seemed, in spite of all efforts, that the typing of the document could not be completed. My thanks go to Mrs. Rita Carlson and Miss Dolores Miller who also shared in the preparation of the document.

There are, however, two people without whose efforts the thesis would

---

[2]"A Note on Interest Rate and the Demand for Money," *Review of Economics and Statistics*, August, 1958.

never have been written. Professor William W. Cooper provided the initial stimulus which caused me to seek a research degree, and since that time he has been unfailingly devoted to my progress toward that degree, and toward the research career beyond it. His aid, encouragement, and patience up to the hour that the document was delivered could not have been exceeded.

Pat, my wife, has given me the support and understanding that enabled me to carry through my intention to complete the dissertation. She worked with me throughout the long nights which accompanied the final stages of the preparation of this thesis.

ANDREW C. STEDRY

Contents

CHAPTER 1

PRELIMINARY CONSIDERATIONS *1*

1.1. *The purpose of control* *1*
1.2. *Budgets: definition and scope* *3*
1.3. *Budgets: standards and standard costs* *5*
1.4. *How a budget controls* *9*
1.5. *Some remarks on budget control and economics* *13*

CHAPTER 2

A MATHEMATICAL MODEL OF A BUDGET CONTROL SYSTEM *17*

2.1. *Introduction* *17*
2.2. *The budget as a determining factor in formation of aspiration levels* *19*
2.3. *Existing models of aspiration level determination* *19*
2.4. *Scope and postulates of the model* *23*
2.5. *Mathematical formulation of the model* *26*
2.6. *Behavior of the system in response to a specific rate of budget reduction* *28*
2.7. *The oscillatory system* *34*
2.8. *A technological constraint* *38*
2.9. *Conclusions* *40*

CHAPTER 3

AVAILABLE EMPIRICAL INFORMATION   *43*

3.1.   *Introduction*   *43*
3.2.   *Laboratory experiments on the level of aspiration*   *43*
3.3.   *Experiments on the behavior of animals*   *50*
3.4.   *Studies of utility measurement*   *52*
3.5.   *Some field studies and a "practical" example*   *56*
3.6.   *Conclusion*   *59*

CHAPTER 4

AN EXPERIMENT   *61*

4.1.   *Introduction*   *61*
4.2.   *The experimental task*   *63*
4.3.   *The reward structure and budget*   *67*
4.4.   *Aspiration level determination*   *71*
4.5.   *Experimental procedure*   *74*
4.6.   *Structure of the design and subjects utilized*   *74*
4.7.   *Analysis of results — performances*   *76*
4.8.   *Analysis of results — aspiration level*   *81*
4.9.   *Conclusions*   *89*

APPENDIX 4A

DETAILS OF THE EXPERIMENTAL DESIGN   *93*

4A.1.   *Task selection*   *93*
4A.2.   *Sample documents*   *95*

APPENDIX 4B

ADDITIONAL STATISTICAL RESULTS   *107*

CHAPTER 5

A MATHEMATICAL MODEL FOR BUDGETARY PLANNING 113

5.1.	*Introduction*	*113*
5.2.	*The hierarchy of the factors of production*	*115*
5.3.	*The concept of limited substitution — a definition*	*116*
5.4.	*Form of the production function under limited substitution*	*117*
5.5.	*Example of a limited substitution problem*	*121*
5.6.	*Computation scheme format*	*127*
5.7.	*Optimization procedure*	*127*
5.8.	*Power of the model*	*136*
5.9.	*Parametric programming of the model*	*139*
5.10.	*Extension of the model to the next higher level in the hierarchy*	*140*
5.11.	*Summary*	*141*

CHAPTER 6

SUMMARY AND DIRECTIONS FOR FURTHER RESEARCH 144

6.1.	*Introduction*	*144*
6.2.	*Planning and control*	*145*
6.3.	*Some selected quotations*	*149*
6.4.	*Some directions for further research*	*154*

	BIBLIOGRAPHY	*155*

CHAPTER 1

Preliminary Considerations

1.1. The Purpose of Control

This is a study in cost control which has as its referent the context of an individual firm where cost reports, budgets, standards, and like mechanics are generally employed to influence cost behavior.[1] It does not deal — or at least it does not deal directly — with those aspects of cost calculation and planning as they bear on problems such as pricing, asset acquisition (and disposition), etc. Because much of the literature in accounting (and practically all of the literature in economics)[2] is devoted to one or the other of these two subjects, it will be useful to try to place this study in the perspective that may be secured by reference to a few pertinent quotations.

Consider, for instance, the following statement as quoted from a report of the National Association of Accountants:[3]

Cost control has as its objective production of the required quality at the lowest possible cost attainable under existing conditions.

Contained in this definition are terms such as "lowest possible,"

---

[1]Specifically, other managed entities such as government agencies, labor unions, etc., are not considered as such. The kind of enterprise which the author has tried to bear in mind is one which is exemplified by a manufacturing firm of the kind which is believed to be typical in America.

[2]A standard reference which is said to go far towards synthesizing economics and accounting is J. M. Clark (19). It will perhaps emphasize what is at issue here by stating that this book has almost nothing to say on those aspects of accounting with which this thesis is concerned.

[3]Formerly the National Association of Cost Accountants. (73a), p. 443.

1

"attainable" and "existing conditions." Although of general applicability, these statements need to be sharpened to render them pertinent here. It is now known, for instance, that under a great variety of situations it is possible to *plan* production without any detailed knowledge of the cost function; existing conditions can be assumed.[1] Does this cost-independent planning ability render the numerous and various kinds of activities that cost accountants normally undertake superfluous insofar as they emanate in cost reports where (numerical) data are presented to those whose primary duty it is to keep costs as low as possible? Under the usual existing conditions — or at least those usually posited in economic theory[2] — this is the case *provided* that, among other things, it is assumed that *plans* are carried forward to their fruition in actual operations. On the other hand, if *control* is the issue so that a mechanism, and especially a mechanism involving human intermediaries, must be considered as the normal way that plans are (possibly) translated into action, then equally severe questions arise as to the standard emphases on "accurate" and timely reports which are art to a common cloth for all recipients of this information.

The usual cost or budget report tends to be a statement of goals in terms of levels; e.g., a standard cost is prescribed, the "actual" level is recorded and variances between the two (possibly) noted. Some consequences of this kind of reporting will be traced in later portions of this thesis (e.g., Chapter 5) and will be shown to give "unwanted" results even when the ideal assumption of exact correspondence between plans and operations can be made. In the earlier portion of this thesis, and in contrast to most of the existing literature, the emphasis will be on rates (or variations between levels in succeeding periods).

In this context the objective of budget control will be given an interpretation which is sharper than the one cited above.[3] As it will be treated here, the objective of budget control is to *increase long-run profit at the fastest possible rate;* or alternatively, at a given output, to *reduce costs at the fastest possible rate.* For the moment, at least, the question of just what rate is the "fastest possible" will be overlooked in order to devote attention to the definition and discussion of the implements of control, the relationship of budget control to the theory of the firm, and a brief description of the development to follow.

---

[1]Cf. F. Modigliani and F. Hohn (62). See also A. Charnes, W. W. Cooper, and B. Mellon (17) and their earlier paper (11).

[2]Specifically, diminishing returns to scale.

[3]It may not even be in accord with what the authors of that report had in mind.

1.2. Budgets: Definition and Scope

In an attempt to eradicate, or at least mitigate, some of the ambiguity which will result from the particular usage of the term "budget" in this thesis, it is necessary to relate it to the definitions in common use. The most comprehensive use of the term is exemplified by the following definition of "budget" by Eric Kohler as:[1]

1. A financial plan serving as a pattern for and a control over future operations;
2. hence, any estimate of future costs;
3. a systematic plan for the utilization of man power, material or other resources.

Implicit in Kohler's definition is the existence of a multiplicity of purposes for which budgets are constructed.

Two major functions are, however, immediately discernable. First, a budget may serve as a *plan*, indicating requirements of certain factors (e.g., cash, productive capacity) at some future date which serves the function of providing information for subsequent decisions and possibly guiding them. Second, a budget may serve as a *control*, containing criteria of cost or performance which will be compared with actual data on operations, thus facilitating evaluations and possible encouraging or even enforcing some measure of efficiency.

As may be already apparent, these separate functions (i.e., planning and controlling) need not be mutually exclusive nor, in practice, is it unusual for both to be represented in a single document. That these functions are (rightly or wrongly) fused is aptly indicated by the following description of "production planning and control" by MacDonald:[2]

> ... one of the essential steps in the preparation of the production budget is the translation of sales estimates into specific production plans. While this activity is primarily the responsibility of the production executive, usually exercised through the head of planning or a production control department, it is so fundamental to practical budgetary control that it is essential that the budget executive at least be familiar with the essential features of it.

There is certainly no doubt indicated in MacDonald's remarks about the advisability, or even necessity, of interlacing the planning and

---

[1](44), p. 67.
[2](53), p. 101.

control functions to the point where they become indistinguishable. A question might be raised, however, as to whether the interrelationship described can, in fact, be achieved with only one set of budgeted figures — a set which would need to serve both planning and control functions at various tiers (and over various persons) in an organization. Consider, for instance, the impact of the following remark as quoted by two other authors.[1] "A good plan (e.g., a budget or sales forecast) does not necessarily yield a good control." Also, "Good planning data and good control data are not necessarily the same."[2] Therefore, it is evident that there is some room for disagreement as well as some need for clarification in these areas, planning and control.

In order to clarify this distinction, reference will be made to sales budgets where it is usual for distinctions of this kind to be recognized in the literature,[3] possibly because widespread divergencies between plans and actual operations are more frequent than in, say, production or financial budgeting. One type of sales budget (frequently termed a "quota") is designed specifically as a control device. Its aims are to effect the motivation and guide the judgment of the salesmen by comparison of budgeted and actual performance. This comparison may (and sometimes is) re-enforced by connection with various rewards and penalties. On the other hand, the tie between these quotas and the planning of output is often extremely loose. The planned output is often based on "estimated" or "expected" sales, and the relations of these expectations to the quotas suggests an assumption that at least some of the quotas will not be achieved.[4] A question arises as to why the "quota" concept is generally not carried over into other areas of budgeting — e.g., production — as a control device. As far as may be discerned, the reasoning is somewhat as follows: the budget must serve as a coordination device. Hence production must be planned so that the needs emanating from "expected sales" will be met along with other criteria, such as the size or fluctuations in inventory, that are regarded as prudent. The assumption which is made in practice (or at least in descriptions of practice) is that the figures to be used for control purposes

---

[1]A. Charnes and W. W. Cooper (11).

[2]*Ibid.*

[3]See, for example, Heckert (34), Chapter 11.

[4]A third figure is sometimes apparent. A sales "forecast" emanating from the sales department may be adjusted downward (to compensate for anticipated optimistic bias) to obtain the sales expectation.

and the estimate of needs (i.e., the production plan) are the same.[1] It is an hypothesis of this thesis that the equality of the figures used for the control and planning budgets need not be assumed, but that its desirability is a testable proposition. Or, in other words, does some figure other than the planned amount, when used in the control budget, produce a performance which is actually closer to the planned amount?

The questions which arise regarding the disparity of plans and controls indicate that the "budget process" is actually not a homogeneous mechanism but rather a collection of processes with a variety of aims and procedures of application. The principles of budgetary practice to be investigated in Chapters 2, 3, and 4 of this thesis concern only the *control* aspects. It may be assumed throughout these chapters that a "budget" can be interpreted as a "control budget" unless otherwise specified. The planning and forecasting aspects of budgeting treated in the thesis are largely contained in Chapter 5 although, as will become evident, the emphasis is on the types of planning considered necessary for adequate control.

1.3. Budgets: Standards and Standard Costs

In order to convey the applicability of the treatment of "budgets" in this paper to control systems using "standards" and "standard costs" as elements of control, the similarity of these various elements will now be discussed. It will first be desirable to examine "standards" and "standard costs" to provide a framework for the discussion of similarities and differences.

Both "standards" and "standard costs" are so intimately related

---

[1]This assumption is typified by some remarks of Rautenstrauch and Villers (64). They state:

> The *yearly production budget* is not equal to the sales forecast, nor to the sales forecast less inventory on hand but to *sales forecasts plus (or minus) the increase (or reduction) of inventory required to bring the actual inventory to the level of budgeted inventory* (p. 114).

This budget is the only one which they propose for control purposes. Note that the distinction between what the budget *is not* and what it *is* is only one which (algebraically) assures that the estimates provide for a continuing enterprise. The possibility that estimated need and the need as stated in the control budget may not agree is not considered. It should be noted in this connection that Professors Rautenstrauch and Villers are industrial engineers. Their views, however, do not differ from those indicated in the citation of Mr. MacDonald (53), an executive, nor markedly from those of Professor Heckert (34) (Chapter 18), an accountant, on the subject of production budgets.

that the one is generally included with the other in any description of cost or profit control mechanisms. It is thus necessary, in order to maintain contact with the main body of accounting literature, to explain the context in which they (i.e., "standards" and "standard costs") will be used in this thesis.

In order to introduce these concepts as they will be used here, the definitions of Eric Kohler will be cited. He defines a *standard* as, "A desired attainment; a performance goal; a model."[1] It will be noted that Kohler views a standard as something to be striven for, and that although various types of schemes are used to set standards, the basic correspondence between standard and goal remains unaltered. Standards are frequently encountered in such specific contexts as "standard time," "standard material usage," etc. In contrast to standard, Kohler defines *standard cost* as, "A forecast or predetermination of what costs should be under projected conditions, serving as a basis for cost control, and as a measure of productive efficiency when ultimately compared with actual costs."[2]

Even with the fairly explicit definitions of Kohler, the problems of classification are not always straightforward. For example, items such as

---

[1](44), p. 389.

[2]*Ibid.* It should be noted that there are several types of standard costs in common use. Since these distinctions are not of prime interest here they will be discussed only briefly. A first classification may be made into two types: *basic standards* and *current standards*. The basic standard is essentially an index number. It is not used for control purposes, other than to exhibit a trend, and frequently is an old standard or actual cost as of a given date, etc. On the other hand, current standards represent the type used in the ordinary context of standards for cost control. These may be set in a variety of ways and may be further subdivided on this basis into two classifications: estimates and standards. Both are expected to relate to current and future production and "the difference between the two is even conceptually a matter of degree. Estimated costs are the looser of the two." (A paraphrase of W. W. Cooper (21), Chapter V, pp. 18-19.)

Additional distinctions, often made, are *ideal* (or *perfection*) *standards* and *attainable standards*. These are both current standards, but the attainable standards are assumed to be able to be obtained under conditions of a reasonable degree of efficiency and effort. They may be either estimates based on past performance or *engineering standards*. The engineering standards are set by time study for labor cost or similar devices for other types of cost. These, too, are in reality estimates, since the standards are often subject to negotiation and there exists no reliable scientific basis upon which to justify an assumption of precision. So-called ideal standards are generally engineering standards, intended to describe the cost that could be attained under "optimum" efficiency. These are the closest to the concept of optimal cost in economic terms, but generally speaking each standard is set individually so that the factor interactions assumed in economic theory are not considered.

"standard labor costs" and "standard material costs" can be classified as "standard costs" and passed by without further discussion, since an absence of ambiguity in these classifications is usually assumed. But what about "standard overhead expense" and like items? Are these a "standard," or a "standard cost"? It is evident that there is some difference in the dimensions, at least as far as control is concerned. Whereas goals or levels used for control which are expressed in units other than dollars are necessarily classed as standards (or budgets, as will be explained later), those which are expressed in dollar terms are frequently classed as standard costs, but not invariably.

In practice, moreover, a "standard time" (expressed in hours) for a particular operation extended by a "standard rate" (cost per hour) for a worker employed on the operation is usually termed a "standard labor cost" for the operation. Any two out of the three figures in this case may serve as the basis for control; the particular pair chosen is a matter of convenience. Conceptually, there is little difference between controlling input or output in physical units as opposed to dollar terms, although they may require different procedures.[1]

From the above comments it may be inferred that the choice of a common denominator — a *numéraire* — is in reality fairly arbitrary, and hence the terms "standard" and "standard cost" can be used more or less interchangeably, at least in a theoretical document of this kind.

Another issue which requires clarification involves the difference between budgets and standards. The distinctions made in the literature vary considerably from author to author so that a concise summary is difficult to achieve. A view which is widely held, however, is that the difference is one of scope. This viewpoint is exemplified in the following remarks of S. Henrici:[2]

> . . . Budgets are customarily set for all departments in the company, from sales to manufacturing. But standards are frequently set only for the manufacturing divisions and can, indeed, be confined to controllable costs in a limited number of cost centers . . .

———

[1]Problems exist, of course, which may definitely indicate preference of one type of unit or the other. In the case of nondivisable joint costs, for example, dollar figures may be misleading. On the other hand, in the control of operations which involve large-scale aggregations of items with a multiplicity of physical units, dollar amounts may provide the only practicable solution.

[2](35), p. 232. A quotation from this same author, to be given shortly, indicates, however, that issues of purpose may also be used to distinguish between "budgeted" and "standard" cost.

Similar statements may be found in Lang, McFarland, and Schiff (46), and Heckert (34), who consider scope the essential difference. Henrici, however, considers scope only one of the distinctions, and not the primary one. He states:

> The first distinction between standards and budgets is one of purpose. Budgets are statements of expected [sic] cost . . . Standards on the other hand, do not necessarily show what costs may be expected to be [sic] but rather what they might be if certain highly desirable performances are attained . . .[1]

On the other hand, I. Wayne Keller proposes a distinction which might well be considered dictated by (in the linguistic sense) "common usage." He writes:[2]

> . . . for control purposes the terms "standard" or "standard cost" are applied to the measurement and control of the costs of direct material, direct labor, and scrap [sic]. Expense is controlled through expense "budgets" rather than expense "standards."

It is apparent from the foregoing conflicting distinctions that no common denominator exists upon which to base a single, well-defined criterion of separation between standards (including standard costs) and budgets. The situation is perhaps best explained by the following statement of the National Association of Accountants' (formerly N.A.C.A.) report, "A Re-Examination of Standard Costs." In relating standard costs to the "scientific management" movement, they note:[3]

> Historically, standard costs as we now know them and business budgeting developed at about the same time, but in the earlier years their development was largely separate. Standard costs developed in the factory while budgeting was applied first to the financial aspect of business. Later on it was realised [sic] that both were merely applications of the same management philosophy and that they were complementary parts of a complete programme of cost control.

This view, which minimizes the difference between budgets and standards, would seem to be most sensible in light of the profusion of conflicting statements which may be found. It also seems, however,

---

[1] *Ibid.* It should be noted that this distinction is not consistent with the definition of Kohler, *supra*, which is used in this paper. (Henrici lists two other distinctions which also depend upon a definition of budget at variance with Kohler's.)

[2] (40), p. 97.

[3] (73a), p. 438.

that planning and forecasting budgets might properly be differentiated from standards, although standards are frequently used in the determination of the plans and forecasts.

On the other hand, a control budget, as defined *supra*, carries with it the connotation of a "goal" or "desired attainment" which is noted in Kohler's definition of standard. It may thus be seen that "budgeted performance" and "standard performance" differ only in name if they are both goals or desired attainments.

Agreement among writers is more or less general only in the matter of the difference in scope exhibited by budgets and standards. It would not be contrary to this consensus if some distinction were made; e.g., a budget is a goal on a large scale, a standard a goal on a smaller scale. But even this distinction would appear to be artificial from the standpoint of classification by function since both a budget and a standard may, in this context, serve the same purpose.

In any case, in this thesis, the meaning of budget (as a control device) will be interpreted as a goal or desired attainment, and the foregoing discussion and quotations used should suffice to justify, to a first approximation, why findings from a study of "budgets" should also be applicable to "standards" or "standard costs" as one or the other (or all three) are used as part of a cost control system.

1.4. How a Budget Controls

In the preceding sections of this chapter, it was noted that there is a control aspect of budgeting that is distinguishable, in some sense, from either planning or forecasting. Assume for the moment that this distinction is valid and can be sufficiently well demarcated; let it then be assumed that a mechanism has been created for the sole purpose of producing and administering a control budget. A question may then be asked as to just what the budget control system and the budget documents (which are an integral part of the system) should consist of in order to insure that the cost or performance elements budgeted are in fact being controlled.

It would seem reasonable that in order to insure some form of control, the process by which control is exercised should be analyzed. In other words, assurance of control would seem to require some answer to the question, "Just how do budgets control?" This issue is rarely addressed in the budgeting literature except by implication and by reference to "experience," "practice," and intuitive appeals that are more or less plausible (when stated).

A more than usually lucid treatment is presented by Henrici. He notes:[1]

> The difference in a given period between actual cost and standard cost, known as the "variance," tells management to what extent costs can be controlled. The variance itself is not a control, for costs are not controlled by compiling statistics about them. The control consists of the steps that management takes to regulate or limit costs. And the effectiveness of these steps is gauged by the degree to which actual costs approach standard; in other words, by the size of the variance.

An important feature to be noted in Henrici's remarks is the absence of the commonly held assumption that the means of reporting and controlling are the same.[2] A second unusual feature is the concept of an approach to standard as a criterion of effectiveness. It should be noted in this regard that Henrici's definition of standard involves a concept not far removed from the "technological optimum" of economics. He considers standards as emphasizing "what *should* be" and having a "primary purpose of establishing a 'sea level,' so to speak, from which to measure cost altitudes."[3] However, standards are frequently set by

---

[1](35), p. 154.

[2]Cf., for example, Lang, McFarland, and Schiff (46), who state, "Control implies the desired objectives through the measurement of results, especially through comparative reports." (p. 435.) Keller (40) likewise appears to overestimate the role of the accounting function. He notes:

> The first requisite for the control of material costs is organization, with responsibilities clearly established for all phases of the control problems. The accountant is the keystone in such an organization, for control will be no better than the accounting records and data which are established. (p. 158)

Both of these authors depend upon the efficiency of their reporting schemes for control. It would seem, however, as though the best reporting scheme would be totally impotent as a control if there were no mechanism for translating reports into action. A *reductio ad absurdum* is sufficient to demonstrate the fallacy in both statements. If both supervisors and budgeted personnel were to ignore all reports — a possibility not excluded by the authors' statements — they would be valueless, regardless of how "good" they were as reports.

[3](35), **p**. 5. But note, however, that there is, within these broad directives, a problem of measurement of standards. Even in the area in which the most extensive work on standards has been performed — the calculation of standard time — the issues are not clear-cut. March and Simon (57) point out that:

> ... Often it is unclear whether standard times reflect "average time using average skill and average effort," "minimum time" or "average time over a series of trials by individuals randomly selected from a pool of industrial workers." (p. 16)

It is thus apparent that, even with the best of intentions, a standard can be misleading.

a criterion which is at best awkwardly paraphrased somewhat as follows: "Standards should be set so that they are 'attainable but not too loose'."[1] If standards are interpreted in terms of this latter criterion, an "approach to standard" implies little more than an approach to a level of performance which was a priori assumed to be approachable, or perhaps more important, capable of betterment.

Returning to the problem of how this approach to standard is to be effected, Henrici's mechanism can be largely considered a search for cause. He assumes that, "Behind every variation from standard cost there is a reason in operating conditions — and very often an apparently good reason."[2] The size and trend of the variances direct supervisory attention to certain phases of activity and the causes of an unfavorable variance are ascertained. These causes are generally assumed to be remediable or nonremediable; "corrective action" is taken in the former case, whereas the latter is dismissed or excused in one form or another.

What has been described above is the essence of so-called "principle of exceptions" or "management by exception." It should be noted that a step has been taken in this thesis in the development of systematic search techniques for the finding and correcting of "remediable causes" of higher costs (or alternatively, lost profit) including the determination of priorities in the order of search. This work is described in Chapter 5. However, the process of "following up" unfavorable variances would seem to be only part of the gain which might be achieved from a system of budgets or standards.

The process of investigation per se places the burden of proof upon management to discover the cause of variances. This is partially transferred to the manager or department head within whose jurisdiction the unfavorable variance occurred; e.g., a report of explanation is required of him so that he must hunt for causes, or at least reasons, to enter in such a report. Often such reports are used to initiate or justify a requested change which, if granted or acceded to by "higher" management, will allow the department head to eliminate or reduce the reported causes of trouble. Alternatively, the report may focus on the existence of some "uncontrollable factor." In principle it may show inefficiency as one root of the difficulty, but here psychological (or economically rational) factors are likely to enter to cloud or obscure matters so that

---

[1]*Vide* Robnett, Hill, and Beckett (66), p. 431; Lang McFarland and Schiff (46), Chapter 16, especially p. 320; and Heckert (34), p. 171 for only a few instances of application of this criterion.

[2](35), p. 154.

recourse must generally be had to other sources; e.g., bolstering of the controls by independent (internal) auditors, special studies, etc. Here again variations in report content as well as differing sources of information are utilized to achieve (or to attempt to achieve) "control."

Consider once more the problem of control as it depends on the motivation (or other psychological and organizational) factors as they affect the person who "causes costs to happen" in the first instance. The process of consideration may well commence with the setting or changing of a standard. The setting of the standard is not sufficient of itself to assure or even invite compliance. The problem of directing activity toward a goal is one of "motivation;" a problem which is ignored, by and large, in the cost accounting and budgeting, except insofar as it deals with issues such as understanding (or the lack thereof) of accounting reports by others. However, as the psychologist Ruch points out, motivation is an integral part of goal-striving activity:[1]

> In any activity there are certain internal conditions or forces *without which there would be no activity* [italics supplied]. These internal conditions [motives] serve to direct the organism toward certain *goals*, regardless of whether these goals are, at the time, present in the organism.

This viewpoint (i.e., when there is no motivation there is no activity) is fundamental to much of psychology. To bring the matter somewhat closer to this thesis, it would appear that Ruch implies that a budget or goal, even if externally imposed, must receive some internal recognition if it is to be at all effective. The following quotation from H. J. Leavitt may be utilized to develop this line of thinking more fully. Professor Leavitt notes:[2]

> No matter how much power a changer may possess, no matter how "superior" he may be, it is the changee who controls the final change decision. It is the employee, even the lowest paid one, who ultimately decides whether to show up for work or not.

It may be perceived from the foregoing remarks that a major area for investigation of the means of budget control involves the relationship between motivations and budgets and standards considered as goals. Chapters 2, 3, and 4 contain the results of an investigation into those aspects of budget control which can be treated as instances of motivated, goal-oriented human behavior.

---

[1](68), p. 105.

[2](49), p. 132.

1.5. Some Remarks on Budget Control and Economics

This is not the place to discuss at length the relation of business practice, budget (and accounting) literature, control, and economic theory. However, remarks are made from time to time on these topics in various parts of this thesis, so it may be well to summarize at least some of the background of these remarks in a more systematic form. First, the theory of economics (at least in its standard form) tends to be oriented towards the analysis of markets, inter- and intra-industry structure, and aggregative types of behavior which are of economy-wide concern. For this reason this theory has little to say about the internal structure of firms or the problems of control that are observed therein.

The model of the firm which economic theory supposes is exceedingly simple, although perhaps adequate for the purposes for which it has been conceived. Briefly, it consists of an "entrepreneur" who makes the basic decisions and certain "factors of production" (e.g., "labor" and "capital") who execute these decisions in faithful detail, and without misunderstanding or possible conflict, to whatever degree approximation is required. All this is done at a price which if paid by the entrepreneur, produces these factors (fully instructed) in whatever quantity the entrepreneur requires. Uncertainty, if introduced into the anlaysis, is never allowed to intervene within the firm, but it is allowed (in many cases) to be a part of the problem with which the entrepreneur must deal as he assesses his external (economics) environment: markets, GNP, and possible actions (or reactions) of his competitors.

Driven usually by an assumed goal of maximum profit (long- or short-run), the entrepreneur chooses a "production function"— a relation which determines the amounts of various factor inputs required to produce the levels of outputs which are deemed desirable by the **entre**preneur. This function, in any given state of technological knowledge, is assumed to be chosen optimally. Various other details then follow, as summarized in the following statement from P. A. Samuelson:[1]

> I. The first fundamental assumption is that the firm tries to maximize its profits, and from this the following internal conditions of equilibrium can be deduced.
>
> A. Any output which is produced must be produced with factor combinations such that total cost is a minimum. As a result of this we have two corollaries.
>
> 1. The marginal productivity of the last dollar must be equal in every use.

---

[1](69), p. 88.

2. The price of each factor of production must be proportional to marginal physical productivity, the factor of proportionality being marginal cost.

B. That output will be selected which maximizes net revenue, total cost being optimally determined by the previous conditions. This implies

1. The equality of marginal cost and marginal revenue, the slope of the latter being the smaller.

2. In combination with previous conditions under A we also have the marginal value productivity of each factor equal to its price, the first term being revenue times marginal physical productivity.

3. Total cost must not exceed total revenue, since otherwise the firm would go out of business.

Evidently this theory is then concerned with certain kinds of machinery for calculating costs as a *prelude* to effecting decisions for *planning* resource allocations and, except for the assumption of faithful and compliant factors, it has little to do in a direct way with the topics of *control* which are primarily at issue in this thesis. Other points may also be made which deal with dynamic as well as static aspects of this theory. However, these are points of increasing refinement, whose pursuit would lead the discussion too far astray. One other general point should be made, however. Under the doctrine of perfect competition there is a control (or at least some aspects of a control) which can be highly effective under certain circumstances. The two important aspects (or rather assumptions of this theory) are as follows: (1) freedom of entry and exit into an industry (anyone may become, or cease to become an entrepreneur), and (2) no firm is sufficiently large so that its actions can have any influence on the prices it pays or receives.

The last of these two assumptions is designed to supply an "impersonal" force without regard (it might be said)[1] to the motivation of the individuals subject to this force. The first admits, under certain plausible conditions, of a series of new entrants who will be attracted into this industry whenever conditions warrant (e.g., because some entrepreneurs are not wholly efficient) and allows not only for new competition from this source but also for competition from already established entrants who may expand their activities at the expense, possibly, of others.[2]

---

[1]It must be assumed that there is always a "sufficient" supply of persons willing to become (or try to become) profit maximizing entrepreneurs. Note, however, that it is not necessary for all entrepreneurs (or potential entrepreneurs) to have this desire. A "marginal" group will, in principle, suffice.

[2]Cf. F. H. Knight (43), pp. 282 ff. for one of the few places where the question of "supply of entrepreneurship" is dealt with.

This means, when translated into administrative terms, that under suitable assumptions each such market enforces (at the top)[1] a rapid series of promotions, demotions, firings, hirings, etc., which along with other penalties and rewards are proportioned to degrees of accomplishment and failure. This is all done in a highly effective and, moreover, impersonal manner whenever these assumptions are fulfilled.

In admiration of this system — or perhaps for other reasons — certain business firms have tried (with more or less success) to import various facsimiles of this system as integral parts of their administrative (and control) mechanisms. The so-called internal profit-and-loss control systems are cases in point.[2] Among other things departments are allowed to deal with each other and with outside entities more or less directly,[3] submitting and receiving bids, negotiating transfer prices, etc., each in the pursuit of its own optimum.

Such systems have not always been successful. On the one hand, it is not always true that the increased efficiency of each department will add up to an increased efficiency of the whole entity (e.g., as measured by profit). On another hand, the assumptions of the theory of perfectly competitive markets have not always been attended to in any careful manner. Moreover, it is by no means clear that they are capable of realization in any place but an "external" market. For instance, there are products within a firm (e.g., those dealing with "work-in-process") which have no readily available sources of supply (or demand) other than different departments within the same firm. Such departments are subject to exploitation by these other departments, at worst, and are insulated from outside pressures, at best. Moreover, departments vary in size, and some may be of such preponderant importance as to vitiate one or both of the key assumptions in a serious way. This again may lead to exploitation or inefficiency, factors which are further reenforced by the appearance of a multiple hierarchy within the firm whose existence has no place in a perfectly competitive market as conceived in economic theory. Finally, the fluidity of entrance and exit which "allows anyone to become an entrepreneur (at the expense, perhaps, of everyone else)" as his own willingness and judgment dictate does not adjust easily to the systems of promotion, demotion, and dismissal found in the hierarchies of most manufacturing firms that are of reasonable size.

---

[1] I.e., at the head of each enterprise.

[2] Cf., for example, Peter Drucker (28) for a description of some of the General Motors Corporation's endeavors in this direction.

[3] E.g., via a central purchasing or sales office.

In any event this economic market theory is not germane, for the most part, to this thesis, except for possible qualifications and points of relevance that will be introduced at appropriate points in the text. Pending their introduction it may be said that the main topic of the thesis is concerned with the effects of goals held by individuals (these will be called aspirations), goals held out for them (or imposed upon them by others), various kinds of reports, and the results these may have for actual performance — immediately and ultimately — under various assumptions.

The presentation will be as follows. In Chapter 2 a mathematical model of a one-cost, one-department budget situation is developed in which the behavior of the individual budgeted is assumed to be a composite of several psychological propositions. Chapter 3 contains descriptions of several experiments with their underlying theories, which are to some extent germane to the study of budget control, and a very limited discussion of a practical application. Chapter 4 contains the description and results of an experiment designed to test some of the assumptions which are made in current budgetary practice and also the assumptions about human behavior upon which the mathematical model of Chapter 2 is based. Chapter 4 also relates the results of the experiment, wherever possible, to the findings of other psychological studies. In Chapter 5, the assumption of a one-cost model is dropped and a model, designed primarily for the purpose of studying the processes of coordination and planning (although having additional implications for control), is presented.

CHAPTER 2

A Mathematical Model of a
Budget Control System

2.1. Introduction

Having established the need for a particular kind of budget whose aim is control, as opposed to planning or forecasting, it is now desirable to investigate the relationship between the control budget figure and actual performance.

To re-emphasize a point made in Chapter 1, a "good" *control* budget is one which produces "good" results. If it is desired to minimize cost in a given department, and if a budget of $1000 produces a cost of $1001, and a budget of $300 produces a cost of $1000, the latter is a better budget. The magnitude of the budget figure is unimportant other than in terms of its impact on cost.

The budget is a goal imposed on an individual, who shall be called a "department head," by his supervisor or supervisors (management). To its attainment are occasionally attached positive rewards, but more frequently, negative rewards are attached to its nonattainment. If it could be assumed that the department head took the budget as his personal goal and worked toward this goal with maximum effort, the criterion of budget control for a single individual would be trivial — i.e., choose a cost goal at the technological minimum for the operation and let him work toward it. It is not difficult to visualize the effects of such a goal in practice. If there is negative reward attached to its non-attainment, some change must be made in the system or the department head will resign, be discouraged, or possibly simply sabotage and oppose

17

the system, perhaps soliciting the help of others to form a group for this purpose.[1] Regardless of the amount of positive reward attached to its attainment, the expected value of reward, statistically speaking, is zero; and the net expected value of rewards and penalties is negative.

In practice the budget may exist on paper at the technological minimum, and doubtless some budget or engineering departments may make just such forecasts for their own guidance. But in actual execution it is usual to secure assent of persons who are to be controlled so that some deviation or adjustment may be applied to this figure. This means that there is some "acceptable" level of cost which, in general, will be above the theoretical optimum. If cost descends below this level the performance is rated as meritorious, but if cost is above this level then there is an implied criticism which may receive explicit form when this fact is called to the department head's attention, and an investigation of causes supplemented by a report (perhaps by outsiders) may ensue. Reprimands, promotion passover, and dismissal are possibilities.

It is a postulate of this thesis that unwritten "acceptable levels" are the common bases of control budgets. Alternatively, there may be an acceptable rate of approach to the technological optimum, which in practice becomes the control element, and the cost level is then determined from the acceptable rate of improvement of the control budget.

Another hypothesis whose logic and empirical content will be investigated is that *a stationary budget[2] is not an effective control budget.* If the budget level is never attained, then some other criterion is in fact replacing it as a control element. If the level is consistently attained, the question of the possibility of consistently obtaining operation at a lower cost will never be answered, because there is no incentive to improve performance. If a level is obtained part of the time, either it must drift toward consistent attainment or nonattainment, or the percentage of the time it will be attained will become stable at some value which produces an acceptable balance of positive and negative reward for the department head. Another and related issue is whether anyone whose performance displays such characteristics would strive for the same reward balance at a lower budgeted cost level. It is part of the task of this thesis to provide a formal basis against which such questions may at least be asked (as they are not in the present literature) and thereby provide a start towards a formal theory of budgetary control. In particular, it is proposed to deal minimally with the question

---

[1] Cf. Argyris (2).

[2] I.e., a budgeted cost for a given operation which does not change over time.

of budgetary level setting in order to focus on the dynamics which center about the question of when (and how) a budget should be changed.

2.2. The Budget as a Determining Factor in Formation of Aspiration Levels[1]

When management presents the department head with a budget, it can only present its goal. It is a hypothesis of this thesis that management can increase the tendency of the department head to aim at or below this goal by increasing the positive reward associated with its attainment and/or increasing the negative reward associated with its nonattainment.

Management can enforce absolute compliance with the budget by dismissal for noncompliance. After this policy has been in effect for a short time, management would retain only the department heads who aimed at or below the budget and were successful at achieving their aims. It would seem, however, that for this procedure to be in operation without a decimation of supervisory personnel, the budget levels would need to be set far above expected cost in order to allow for random fluctuations. Such a procedure seems unlikely to cause the department head to drive his costs far below the budget, since safety will take priority over innovation. The fear of a lowering of the budget if he performs too well will undoubtedly dominate a desire to impress management with superior performance.[2] Barring this undesirable procedure, the budget may be considered at best a candidate for the department head's goal but more generally as one factor which operates in its determination. This level of cost toward which the department head strives will be termed his *aspiration level*.

2.3. Existing Models of Aspiration Level Determination

The definition of aspiration level which will be used here is consistent with the definition of J. D. Frank: "The level of future performance in a familiar task which an individual, knowing his level of past performance in that task, explicitly undertakes to reach."[3] Considerable documentation, both theoretical and empirical, is available for the existence of

---

[1]My initial contact with aspiration levels was aided immensely by William H. Starbuck and his excellent survey of the field (74). The mathematical formulations of this section (before budget impositions) are contained in that paper.

[2]Cf. Barnard (3), particularly pp. 149-153.

[3]J. D. Frank (33), p. 119.

aspiration levels in the absence of explicit external goals. For example, Lewin, Dembo, Festinger, and Sears[1] have hypothesized a model in which they define as the basic reference variable, x, the level of difficulty. The probability of success, $P(x)$, is the subjective probability of achieving a level of performance of equal or greater difficulty than x. The utility of success, $S(x)$, and the utility of failure, $F(x)$, are assumed to be monotone increasing and decreasing functions of x, respectively. The level of aspiration, A, is that level of difficulty which maximizes $V(x)$, where

(2.3.1) $$V(x) = P(x) \cdot S(x) + [1 - P(x)] \cdot F(x)$$

If x is a monotone decreasing function of c, the cost level, then this utility maximization could conceivably be used to find the aspired cost level. In the industrial context, however, it is difficult — almost impossible — to envision a situation in which a department head does not perceive some sort of external goal whether or not explicitly stated. Imposing upon the Lewin *et al.* model the cost transformation and a budget level, b, for which reward is administered on a go no-go basis produces the following discontinuous utility function:

(2.3.2) $$\begin{aligned} V(c) &= P(c) \cdot S(c) + [1 - P(c)] \cdot F(c) + R &\qquad c \leq b \\ &= P(c) \cdot S(c) + [1 - P(c)] \cdot F(c) + P &\qquad c > b \end{aligned}$$

where R is the utility of reward for attaining the budget, P the disutility of the punishment for not attaining the budget, and $P(c)$ is the probability of a cost level less than or equal to c. The point of maximum expected utility (the aspiration level) of the discontinuous function will occur at the same point, A, as that of the continuous function (i.e., $R = P = 0$) if $b > A$ (in which case the budget is superfluous), or if $b \leq A$ and $R - P$ is less than the difference between $V(A)$ and $V(b)$ calculated for $R = P = 0$ (which generally speaking will result if the subjective probability of success at the budgeted level is small relative to the reward for attaining it). Otherwise the aspiration and budget levels will coincide.[2]

---

[1]See (37b) pp. 356-377 but especially pp. 360-361; and also for further discussion of the model, Starbuck (74), pp. 1-3.

[2]The aspiration level need not be single valued. If $V(b)_{R,P=0} = V(A)_{R,P,=0}$ $b < A$, two values appear:

$$a = b$$
$$a = A$$

Although, mathematically, this case occurs with zero probability, the range of indifference between b and A as aspirations is undoubtedly finite and perhaps large in practice.

An obvious implication of the augmented Lewin model is that management can equate aspiration and budget levels for sufficiently large but finite $R - P$, at *any* value of the budget including (unfortunately) $b = 0$ (unless $F(0) = -\infty$, which would render the entire model meaningless). The model also implies that either the aspiration level is equal to the budget or is completely independent of it. This conclusion stems from the go no-go character assumed for reward; the more reasonable belief that an individual's aspiration is affected by the budget even if the two are unequal stems from the implicit assumption that the reward-penalty structure produces discontinuities in the utility function at more than one point and that the locations of the additional points depend upon the budget. Proliferation of these points of discontinuity would provide an aspiration level at one of them or at A. With the exception of the allowance of an aspiration level of zero cost, the augmented Lewin model predicts plausible behavior of the aspiration level in response to a budget.

The difficulties of the Lewin model for this exposition are twofold. First, it falls short of supplying all of the required characteristics for operational significance in that it provides no means of predicting actual behavior. Secondly, the reliance on subjective probabilities makes it more difficult operationally to predict the aspiration level than to measure it. These difficulties preclude the adoption of the Lewin model for the purposes of this chapter. The implications of the model to be presented below are, however, consistent with those of the Lewin model.

Two models, one of Simon[1] and one of March and Simon,[2] utilize the availability of alternatives as a factor in the determination of aspiration levels.

In the Simon model, phrased in the terminology of the augmented Lewin model,

(2.3.3)
$$V(c) < 0 \text{ for } c > a$$
$$V(c) > 0 \text{ for } c < a$$

where a is the aspiration level in terms of the aspired cost level. Essentially, Simon assumes that individuals do not maximize utility, but merely search until a satisfactory goal (one with positive utility) is found, and then cease to search. The aspiration level then is the last goal found by the search process; all earlier goals encountered are

---

[1] See *Models of Man* (72), pp. 241-260. The mathematical formulation of the model in Lewin terminology is due to Starbuck (74).

[2] March-Simon (57), p. 48.

unsatisfactory (possess negative utility). According to this hypothesis, if the budget (which is an alternative which requires no search) possesses a positive utility, the department head will adopt it as his aspiration level. Using the expected utility function of the augmented Lewin model (2.3.2), it is noted that the Simon model equates the aspiration and budget levels in every case that the Lewin model does unless $V(c) < 0$ for all c (in which case the Simon model has no solution for the aspiration level while the Lewin model has a solution which may equate a and b), and also some in which the Lewin model would choose $a = A$ (i.e., $V(A) > V(b) > 0$). The Simon model, like the Lewin model, gives no clue as to the reaction of performance to changes in aspirations. Furthermore, since it does not specify the method of search if $V(b) < 0$, it leads to the completely plausible but operationally limited conclusion that either aspiration level equals the budget level or is unknown.

The March-Simon model is, to my knowledge, the only existing dynamic model of aspiration level determination. It can be summarized in the four equations:[1]

$$(2.3.4) \quad
\begin{array}{lll}
\text{(a)} & \dfrac{dA}{dt} = \alpha(R - A + a), & a > 0,\ \alpha > 0 \\[2ex]
\text{(b)} & S = R - A & \\[1ex]
\text{(c)} & L = \beta(\overline{S} - S) & \overline{S} > 0,\ \beta > 0 \\[2ex]
\text{(d)} & \dfrac{dR}{dt} = \alpha(L - b - cR) & \alpha > 0,\ b \geq 0,\ c > 0
\end{array}$$

where $S \equiv$ satisfaction, $A \equiv$ level of aspiration, $L \equiv$ search rate, $R \equiv$ expected value of reward, and $\overline{S} \equiv$ desired level of satisfaction. The system possesses a stable equilibrium solution:

$$(2.3.5) \quad
\begin{array}{ll}
\text{(a)} & A = R + a \\[1ex]
\text{(b)} & L = b + cR
\end{array}$$

It is to be noted that the aspiration level can be interpreted as aspired reward, as opposed to the other models in which aspiration level is related to a performance level or the difficulty of its achievement. It is much more reasonable to assume that the *long-run* aspirations of an individual whose behavior these various models attempt to describe relate to his ultimate compensation rather than his performance. However, in the absence of some way of relating the level of search effort to a measurable set of criteria, the above model is of limited usefulness as a basis for the principles of a theory of budgetary control.

Although the above discussion is not by any means an exhaustive

---

[1] *Ibid.*

coverage of aspiration level models, I have described those which I feel have the greatest applicability to aspiration level formulation with the complication of an external goal. Each, however, lacks at least one essential attribute for the present task of relating aspiration levels, external goals, and actual performance. I therefore proceed to the development of a new model which occasionally borrows from the ones described in this section and, wherever possible, is consistent with them.

2.4. Scope and Postulates of the Model

The aim of this model is to provide a vehicle for establishing rules for optimum management policy with regard to the setting of budgets for a single department. The choice of a one-department model requires for its validity an amendment to the definition of Chapter 1 which would allow a "sub-budget" of the budget control system for the enterprise to be considered by itself. This dissection leaves out many interesting and significant questions concerned with interdepartmental reactions and therefore some of the *raison d'être* for the existence of a central budgetary office. Some of the facets of the interrelationships will be treated in Chapter 5, but are omitted here for the purpose of investigation of the unicellular case whose behavior is as yet incompletely determinate.

It is assumed that the accounting system and the budget are so devised that the behavior of cost in a single cost-incurring unit may be considered *ceteris paribus*. That is, a department head can be held fully responsible for the costs incurred; overhead costs for which he cannot be held accountable, variations in production level which are not of his making, etc. have been removed from the calculation of cost. There is, incidentally, considerable indication that the accounting procedures for measurement of costs and the allocation of responsibility for them are highly developed,[1] and that a single *ceteris paribus* cost figure can be attributed to the operations of a particular man in the organization who will generally accept responsibility for its fluctuations. The problem which is at issue here is not in ascertaining what costs *are*, but what goals are to be set for them and how the cost performance should be evaluated. It is further assumed that the costs discussed here either (1) occur under invariant output or (2) have been adjusted independently for variations in output.

Three interrelated cost levels are relevant to the system. The

---

[1]See, for example, Lasser (48), p. 34.

budgeted level of expenditure is that level which is set by higher management. The cost level which the department head strives to achieve — the aspired level — is dependent upon the budgeted level, but is not necessarily equal to that level. The level of expenditure which the accounting system shows to have actually taken place (perhaps refined, as indicated in the preceding paragraph) will be known simply as the expected actual cost level, or more simply, the cost level.

The level of expenditure is in units of dollars per fixed accounting period; e.g., dollars per year. However, the level of expenditure can be determined at any instant of time; i.e., it is the instantaneous rate of flow of expenditures.

The assumptions of the model can best be comprehended in the following set of postulates for the behavior of a hypothesized department head.

(i)   If there is a *discrepancy* between the *expected actual level of expenditure* and the *aspired level of expenditure*, he will attempt to reduce this discrepancy by moving his aspiration level toward the actual level at a rate which depends on the size of the discrepancy.

(ii)   In addition to the effect caused by the discrepancy, the *aspired level of expenditure* will be lowered in response to a lowering of the *budgeted level of expenditure*.

(iiia) The department head will be *encouraged* if the discrepancy (actual expected cost minus aspired cost) does not exceed some positive value known as the *discouragement point*.

(iiib) The department head will be *discouraged* if the discrepancy exceeds the *discouragement point* but does not exceed a larger value known as the *failure point*.

(iiic) If the value of the discrepancy exceeds the *failure point*, the system will cease to exist, or a new one will come into being; "the department head will resign."

(iva)   If the department head is *encouraged*, he will attempt to reduce a positive discrepancy by reducing the *expected actual level of expenditure;* he will react to a negative discrepancy by allowing expected cost to rise.[1] The rate of reduction or increase depends upon the size of the discrepancy.

---

[1] If a multiple commodity or multiple cost structure was hypothesized, it would be assumed that negative stress in one area would direct attention to another. Cf. Edwards (30), and note Chapter 3, p. 54, of this thesis.

(ivb)   If the department head is *slightly discouraged*, he will reduce the discrepancy by reducing expected cost at a lower rate relative to a given discrepancy than he would if encouraged. If he is *moderately discouraged*, he will allow expected cost to increase, but at a sufficiently small rate that the discrepancy will not be increased. If he is *extremely discouraged*, he will allow expected cost to increase at a rate which increases the discrepancy.

Postulate (ii) describes a situation in which the budget is a figure about which there are several auxiliary points, each of which defines a particular set of rewards. Using the Simon model of aspiration level determination, the department head will find a point at which the rewards are "satisfactory." He will then study the relationship of this point to the budget, find out about how much it changes for a given change in the budget, and then change his aspiration level accordingly, responding to changes in the budget. Postulate (i) is essentially Lewinian in nature, in that the department head may be interpreted as responding to a positive discrepancy as a reduction of the perceived probability of success of the original aspiration, adjusting his aspiration level in the direction of increased probability of success. The discrepancy between the expected actual level of expenditure and the aspired level of expenditure is appropriately termed a measure of *stress*, since clearly the department head's "emotional tension, produced by frustration,"[1] varies with the size of the discrepancy. A compromising of goals is a well-known reaction to stress,[2] and hence postulate (i) may be interpreted directly as a stress-reducing mechanism without considering the existence of subjective probabilities.

Postulate (iva) describes the department head as exhibiting another "normal" form of reaction to stress — striving to improve performance. A primary assumption of this model is that man is an improvable animal and that, given sufficient motivation, cost reduction is a possibility. March and Simon (57) have confined their discussion of improvement to an increase in search behavior.[3] It is assumed here that improvement is possible through increased experience with the task, diverting of effort from nonorganizational goals, development of increased "cost-consciousness" (diverting of effort from other organizational goals in

---

[1]F. S. Ruch (68), p. 154.

[2]*Ibid.*, p. 162.

[3]But Cf. *Handbook of Experimental Psychology*, Chapter 13, Neal E. Miller, "Learnable Drives and Rewards," where this same kind of search for improved situations is ascribable to fear and anxiety (78a).

which there is less stress), or mere harder work — all of which may be considered part of or in addition to search behavior. Postulate (iiia) notes a limitation on the amount of stress which the department head can tolerate and still devote his efforts to cost reduction at maximum effectiveness.

Postulate (ivb) describes the various stages of withdrawal within the range of stress denoted by postulate (iiib). Caused by sublimation or ineffective effort due to stereotypy of response, the department head will be less successful in reducing costs. The neurotic response of extreme discouragement will eventually lead to ultimate withdrawal (postulate (iiic)), provided some change does not occur within the system. The assumption that exceeding the discouragement point will evoke one of only three types of behavior depending on the individual department head is made for the sake of simplicity rather than necessity.

2.5. Mathematical Formulation of the Model

An analytic statement will help to clarify what is involved in the preceding postulates, and for this purpose it will be assumed that the relationships between the variables are linear. Let c = expected actual level of expenditure, a = aspired level of expenditure and b = budgeted level of expenditure. Then

$$(2.5.1) \qquad \frac{da}{dt} = \beta(c - a) + \gamma \frac{db}{dt} \qquad \text{where } \beta > 0,\ \gamma \geq 0$$

describes the relationships of postulates (i) and (ii), and

$$(2.5.2) \qquad \frac{dc}{dt} = -\alpha_i(c - a) \qquad \text{where } i = 1,\ 2 \text{ and } \alpha_1 > \alpha_2,\ \alpha_1 \geq 0$$

describes the relationships of postulates (iva) and (ivb) with the exception of limitations on α_2.

Let M = the discouragement point and N = the failure point. The constants of (2.5.2) can then be qualified as

$(2.5.3a)$ $\alpha_i = \alpha_1$ where $c - a \leq M$ (postulate iiia)

$(2.5.3b)$ $\alpha_i = \alpha_2$ where $M < c - a \leq N$ (postulate iiib) and

$(2.5.3c)$ α_i not defined   where $N < c - a$ (postulate iiic)

for $M,\ N > 0$ and finite. The state of discouragement depends upon β as well as α_2 in the following manner:

(2.5.4a) if $\beta + \alpha_2 > \alpha_2 \geq 0$ he is slightly discouraged

(2.5.4b) if $\beta + \alpha_2 \geq 0 > \alpha_2$ he is moderately discouraged and

(2.5.4c) if $0 > \beta + \alpha_2 \geq \alpha_2$ he is extremely discouraged

in accordance with postulate (ivb).

This completes the mathematical formulation of the system.

An assumption which will be made about management budget behavior is

$$(2.5.5) \qquad \frac{db}{dt} = -K_j \qquad (j = 1, \cdots, n)$$

which postulates a constant rate of budget reduction which can be changed to another rate by a *management decision*. That is $j = 1, 2, \cdots$, n represents the set of decision possibilities with respect to rates of budget reduction. Note that db/dt is (at least in part) controlled by persons beyond the authority of the affected manager.

Provided either of the conditions (2.5.3a) or (2.5.3b) are met and no management decisions occur for all t, denoting the initial values of the variables by a zero subscript, the solutions to the system of equations (2.5.1) and (2.5.2) are

$$(2.5.6a) \qquad c = c_0 e^{-(\beta+\alpha_i)t} + \frac{\alpha_i a_0 + \beta c_0}{\beta + \alpha_i}[1 - e^{-(\beta+\alpha_i)t}]$$

$$- \frac{\alpha_i \gamma K_j}{(\beta + \alpha_i)^2}[e^{-(\beta+\alpha_i)t} + (\beta + \alpha_i)t - 1]$$

$$a = a_0 e^{-(\beta+\alpha_i)t} + \frac{\alpha_i a_0 + \beta c_0}{\beta + \alpha_i}[1 - e^{-(\beta+\alpha_i)t}]$$

$$(2.5.6b) \qquad - \frac{\alpha_i \gamma K_j}{(\beta + \alpha_i)}t - \frac{\beta \gamma K_j}{(\beta + \alpha_i)^2}[1 - e^{-(\beta+\alpha_i)t}]$$

The system possesses a stable equilibrium if and only if $\gamma K_j = 0$, which will result either if the budget is static or if the department head completely ignores its changes. In this case, the equilibrium solution is

$$(2.5.7) \qquad \lim_{t \to \infty} c = \lim_{t \to \infty} a = \frac{\alpha_i a_0 + \beta c_0}{\beta + \alpha_i}$$

provided, of course, that no changes in the department head's state of encouragement or management decisions take place.

However, a basis for defining the behavior of the system as t grows large exists since

$$(2.5.8) \quad \frac{dc}{dt} = - \alpha_i(c - a)$$

$$= - \alpha_i(c_0 - a_0)e^{-(\beta+\alpha_i)t} - \frac{\alpha_i \gamma K_j}{\beta + \alpha_i}[1 - e^{-(\beta+\alpha_i)t}]$$

possesses a limit provided that $(\beta + \alpha_1) > 0$. Specifically

$$(2.5.9) \qquad \lim_{t \to \infty} \frac{dc}{dt} = - \frac{\alpha_i \gamma K_j}{\beta + \alpha_i}$$

Note, then, from the last expression that external (e.g., central) management can produce an effect on cost behavior even when $a_0 = c_0$. Also, the expression (2.5.9) suggests the usefulness of an equilibrium *rate* for the case dc/dt and da/dt constant. In terms of such an equilibrium $(\beta + \alpha_i)$ may be regarded as the "speed of adjustment" or "time constant;" i.e., the rate at which dc/dt approaches rate equilibrium. (A constant dc/dt implies constant da/dt and conversely, so that it will only be necessary to discuss dc/dt.)

2.6. Behavior of the System in Response to a Specific Rate of Budget Reduction

A system which can attain a condition of rate equilibrium in a state (of encouragement or discouragement) will be considered *rate stable* in that state. A system in a given state which is both rate stable in that state and for which

$$(2.6.1) \qquad \lim_{t \to \infty} \frac{dc}{dt} \leq 0$$

will be designated an *admissible system*. By definition, an admissible system is a sufficient condition for nonincreasing costs in the limit. In order to show that an admissible system is also a necessary condition, it must be shown that dc/dt is bounded below.[1] If $\beta + \alpha_i > \alpha_i \geq 0$, as in the encouraged state and the slightly discouraged state, the relations $\alpha_i \geq 0$ and $(c - a) \leq N$, ensure that[2]

$$(2.6.2) \qquad \frac{dc}{dt} = - \alpha_i(c - a) \geq - \alpha_i N$$

On the other hand, if $\beta + \alpha_2 \geq 0 > \alpha_2$, as in the moderately discouraged state, then

$$(2.6.3) \qquad \frac{dc}{dt} = \alpha_2(a - c) \geq \alpha_2(-N) > 0.$$

---

[1]Otherwise, the possibility would exist that a system which possesses no rate equilibrium solution could exhibit cost reduction at an ever-increasing rate.

[2]It is interesting to note that should the pathological case $c - a < 0$ exist, then dc/dt is everywhere non-negative. If $\alpha_1 < 0$ were allowed, however, this nonnegativity would not hold and, in fact, dc/dt would not be bounded below.

The extremely discouraged state is likewise devoid of admissible systems since

$$(2.6.4) \qquad \frac{dc}{dt} = \alpha_2(a - c) = (-\alpha_2)(c - a) > (-\alpha_2)M > 0.$$

It follows immediately that if a system remains in a state but does not possess rate stability in that state, dc/dt, since it must then be unlimited but bounded below, will increase without bound. Thus an admissible system is both a necessary and sufficient condition for nonincreasing costs in the limit.

If the department head is initially encouraged, which means that the initial spread between actual and aspired cost behavior is sufficiently small, the system will come to rest in the encouraged state if management does not attempt to reduce costs at too great a rate. That is, if management chooses to keep the department head encouraged it will choose a rate of budget reduction K_j such that

$$(2.6.5) \qquad 0 \leq \gamma K_j \leq (\beta + \alpha_1) M$$

Since $\beta + \alpha_1$ has been assumed non-negative

$$(2.6.6a) \qquad c - a = (c_0 - a_0)e^{-(\beta+\alpha_1)t} + \frac{\gamma K_j}{(\beta + \alpha_1)} [1 - e^{-(\beta+\alpha_1)t}]$$

$$(2.6.6b) \qquad \leq (c_0 - a_0 - M)[e^{-(\beta+\alpha_1)t}] + M$$

$$(2.6.6c) \qquad \leq M$$

Not only is management thus assured of keeping the department head encouraged, but it is also assured, in the long run, of a constant rate of cost *reduction* since

$$(2.6.7) \qquad \lim_{t\to\infty} \frac{dc}{dt} = -\frac{\alpha_1\gamma K}{\beta + \alpha_1} \leq 0,$$

which clearly describes an admissible system. If the first weak inequality in (2.6.5) is replaced by the stronger condition of strict inequality then a nontrivial admissible solution is assured.[1]

If, however, management elects a high rate of cost reduction, seen by the department head to be "intolerable," viz.

$$(2.6.8) \qquad \gamma K_j > (\beta + \alpha_1) M$$

---

[1]This obviously requires positive γ as well; i.e., some degree of acquiescence from the department head. Cf., pp. 9–12.

the solution obtained for t by equating equation (2.6.6a) to M,

$$(2.6.9) \qquad \tau_1 = \frac{1}{\beta + \alpha_1} \ln \left[\frac{\gamma K_j - (\beta + \alpha_1)(c_0 - a_0)}{\gamma K_j - (\beta + \alpha_1) M} \right]$$

is non-negative, since

$$(2.6.10) \quad \gamma K_j - (\beta + \alpha_1)(c_0 - a_0) \geq \gamma K_j - (\beta + \alpha_1) M > 0$$

The trivial solution, $\tau_1 = 0$, (immediate transition to discouragement) can occur only if the initial conditions place $c_0 - a_0$ precisely at the discouragement point M. A non-negative solution for (2.6.9) implies that the system will undergo a transition to the discouraged state immediately or after a finite time, τ_1.

If the department head is initially discouraged ($N \geq (c_0 - a_0) > M$), the conditions for rest and transition are dependent on the level of discouragement. If the department head becomes extremely discouraged, and if management unwisely applies a rate K_j such that

$$(2.6.11) \qquad\qquad \gamma K_j \geq (\beta + \alpha_2)(c_0 - a_0)$$

then it can defeat its own purpose and *cause* a cost increase. This occurs because

$$(2.6.12) \quad c - a = (c_0 - a_0)e^{-(\beta + \alpha_2)t} + \frac{\gamma K_j}{\beta + \alpha_2} [1 - e^{-(\beta + \alpha_2)t}]$$

$$= \left(c_0 - a_0 - \frac{\gamma K_j}{\beta + \alpha_2} \right) e^{-(\beta + \alpha_2)t} + \frac{\gamma K_j}{\beta + \alpha_2}$$

is an increasing function of time. Furthermore, equating equation (2.6.12) to N gives a non-negative solution for t, analogous to the discussion of (2.6.9) above, except that the relevant summary of conditions is

$$(2.6.13) \quad \gamma K_j - (\beta + \alpha_2)N \geq \gamma K_j - (\beta + \alpha_2)(c_0 - a_0) \geq 0 > \beta + \alpha_2$$

Hence, the management behavior shown in (2.6.11) assures the eventual failure of the system — i.e., "the department head will leave the organization" — and does so under the adverse condition (for management) of causing an increase in costs to bring this eventuality about. If management wishes to avoid the transition from extreme discouragement to failure, it must choose a rate of budget *increase* which is sufficiently large to overcome the disequilibrium-producing behavior of the department head and the initial discrepancy; namely,

$$(2.6.14) \qquad \gamma K_j < (\beta + \alpha_2)(c_0 - a_0) < (\beta + \alpha_2)M < 0$$

The second and third strong inequalities are required by the negativity and the initial conditions. In equation (2.6.14) implies

$$(2.6.15) \quad \beta + \alpha_2 < 0 < (\beta + \alpha_2)(c_0 - a_0) - \gamma K_j < (\beta + \alpha_2) - \gamma K_j$$

which insures a positive solution for t to $c - a = M$ which is

$$(2.6.16) \qquad \tau_2 = \frac{1}{\beta + \alpha_2} \ln \left[\frac{(\beta + \alpha_2)(c_0 - a_0) - \gamma K_j}{(\beta + \alpha_2) M - \gamma K_j} \right]$$

which in turn implies a transition to the encouraged state.

In summary, under the indicated conditions, management can adopt either one of two alternatives which are better than the one indicated. It can force such an extremely discouraged department head to resign and thereby at least avoid the cost increases which would otherwise produce this eventuality anyway; or also it can undertake a restoration of the department head's confidence by granting him a large budget increase. No intermediate solution exists.

It must not be assumed, however, that management can either act arbitrarily or ignore the cost consequences attendant on budget changes for the slightly or moderately discouraged department head. Management can still cause system failure by choosing a rate such that

$$(2.6.17) \qquad \qquad \gamma K_j > (\beta + \alpha_2) N$$

The proof of transition to failure is precisely the same as for the transition to discouragement above with N and α_2 substituted for M and α_1, respectively. The parameter values of α and β are, of course, vitally important. By making the same substitutions, it can be shown that failure is impossible, given

$$(2.6.18) \qquad \qquad (\beta + \alpha_2) N \geq \gamma K_j \geq (\beta + \alpha_2) M$$

The second half of the inequality implies

$$
\begin{aligned}
c - a &= \left[c_0 - a_0 - \frac{\gamma K_j}{\beta + \alpha_2} \right] e^{-(\beta + \alpha_2)t} + \frac{\gamma K_j}{\beta + \alpha_2} \\
&\geq \left[c_0 - a_0 - \frac{\gamma K_j}{\beta + \alpha_2} \right] e^{-(\beta + \alpha_2)t} + M \\
&\geq \left[M - \frac{\gamma K_j}{\beta + \alpha_2} \right] e^{-(\beta + \alpha_2)t} + M \\
&\geq M
\end{aligned}
$$

(2.6.19)

Thus the system will come to rest in the discouraged state with

$$(2.6.20) \qquad \lim_{t \to \infty} \frac{dc}{dt} = - \frac{\alpha_2 \gamma K_j}{\beta + \alpha_2}$$

which will be an admissible solution if the department head is only slightly discouraged, inadmissible otherwise. Without further laboring the point, equation (2.6.16) is a positive solution for t of the equation $c - a = M$, assuring transition to the encouraged state provided that

$$(2.6.21) \qquad \gamma K_j < (\beta + \alpha_2) M$$

which becomes

$$(2.6.22) \quad (\beta + \alpha_2)(c_0 - a_0) - \gamma K > (\beta + \alpha_2) M - \gamma K > 0$$

With the moderately discouraged department head no admissible solution is available so that the permissive procedure shown in (2.6.21) is advantageous. The slightly discouraged department head, however, may perform better in the discouraged state if his failure point is sufficiently high.

Specifically, if in the slightly discouraged case, $N > \dfrac{\alpha_1 M}{\alpha_2}$, K_j can be chosen such that

$$(2.6.23) \qquad (\beta + \alpha_2)N \geq \gamma K_j > \frac{\alpha_1}{\alpha_2} (\beta + \alpha_2)M$$

Clearly this condition and $\alpha_1 \geq \alpha_2 \geq 0$ insures fulfillment of inequation (2.6.18), the condition for rest in the discouraged state,[1] with an admissible solution given by

$$(2.6.24) \qquad \lim_{t \to \infty} \frac{dc}{dt} = - \frac{\alpha_2 \gamma K_j}{\beta + \alpha_2} < - \alpha_1 M$$

In the encouraged state the condition for rest, inequation (2.6.5), implies that the rate-equilibrium value of cost reduction has a lower bound; namely

$$(2.6.25) \qquad \lim_{t \to \infty} \frac{dc}{dt} = - \frac{\alpha_1 \gamma K}{\beta + \alpha_1} \geq - \alpha_1 M$$

---

[1]It is also relevant that $\alpha_2 \geq 0$ implies

$$\frac{\alpha_1}{\alpha_2} (\beta + \alpha_2) - (\beta + \alpha_1) = \frac{\beta(\alpha_1 - \alpha_2)}{\alpha_2} \geq 0$$

so that a K which satisfies (2.6.23) also satisfies (2.6.8), the condition for transition to discouragement, assuring the attainment of the best solution shown in (2.6.24) independent of initial conditions.

indicating that a higher rate of cost reduction is possible in the discouraged state. This policy might be considered "hard-boiled" or even unscrupulous, but the rate of budget reduction for the man who becomes only slightly discouraged and gives up completely only under extreme provocation should be calculated to keep him just short of resignation at all times.

To bring some of the points already discussed together in a convenient form, the results of the various management actions are summarized in Table 2.1.

TABLE 2.1

Initial State	Management Action	System Reaction*
encouraged	$\gamma K_j > (\beta + \alpha_1)M$	$\rightarrow$ discouragement
	$0 \le \gamma K_j \le (\beta + \alpha_1)M$	admissible rest (best solution if $N \le \frac{\alpha_1}{\alpha_2}M$ or $\alpha_2 < 0$)
slightly discouraged	$\gamma K_j > (\beta + \alpha_2)N$	$\rightarrow$ failure
	$(\beta + \alpha_2)N \ge \gamma K_j \ge (\beta + \alpha_2)M$	admissible rest (best solution if $N > \frac{\alpha_1}{\alpha_2}M$)
	$\gamma K_j < (\beta + \alpha_2)M$	$\rightarrow$ encouraged
moderately discouraged	$\gamma K_j > (\beta + \alpha_2)N$	$\rightarrow$ failure
	$(\beta + \alpha_2)N \ge \gamma K_j \ge (\beta + \alpha_2)M$	rest — not admissible
	$\gamma K_j < (\beta + \alpha_2)M$	$\rightarrow$ encouraged
extremely discouraged	$\gamma K_j \ge (\beta + \alpha_2)(c_0 - a_0)$	$\rightarrow$ failure
	$\gamma K_j < (\beta + \alpha_2)(c_0 - a_0) < (\beta + \alpha_2)M$	$\rightarrow$ encouraged

*The symbol $\rightarrow$ represents "transition to."

If management chooses to restrict itself to only one level of cost reduction, the system must come to rest in its initial state, come to rest after a single transition, or fail.

The condition for the encouraged $\rightarrow$ discouraged transition given by (2.6.8) implies

$$(2.6.26) \qquad \gamma K_j > (\beta + \alpha_1)M > (\beta + \alpha_2)M$$

which would satisfy either the condition (2.6.18) for coming to rest in the discouraged state or one of the failure conditions (2.6.11) or (2.6.17). Similarly, either of the discouraged $\rightarrow$ encouraged transition conditions (2.6.14) or (2.6.21) would imply

$$(2.6.27) \qquad \gamma K < (\beta + \alpha_2)M < (\beta + \alpha_1)M$$

which is sufficient for coming to rest in the encouraged state.

The discussion to this point has been oriented towards asymptotic behavior. If no oscillation is allowed — since solutions which are not rate-stable lead to system failure — the discussion of optimal behavior may be restricted to systems at rest. If the department head is initially encouraged, and the discouragement level is moderate or extreme (or slight but with $N \leq \frac{\alpha_1}{\alpha_2}M$) then the optimal behavior and resultant rate of change of cost are given by

$$(2.6.28) \qquad\qquad K_j = \frac{(\beta + \alpha_1)M}{\gamma}$$

$$\frac{dc}{dt} = -\alpha_1 M$$

If the discouragement level is slight and $N > \frac{\alpha_1}{\alpha_2}M$, optimal behavior and resultant change of cost are given by:

$$(2.6.29) \qquad\qquad K_j = \frac{(\beta + \alpha_2)N}{\gamma}$$

$$\frac{dc}{dt} = -\alpha_2 N$$

independent of initial conditions.

If the level of discouragement is moderate or extreme and the department head is initially discouraged, management has no satisfactory single K_j.[1] If this is the case or, in fact, if discouragement is slight and $N \leq \frac{\alpha_1}{\alpha_2}M$, management should initially apply a rate which is sufficiently small to cause a transition to encouragement and then shift to the rate shown in (2.6.28). Since this second rate assures coming to rest in the encouraged state, the condition of nonoscillation is not violated by the shift in rate.

2.7. The Oscillatory System

It would appear at first glance that management could decrease the budget rapidly, causing a large reduction in cost and subsequently "take off the pressure," allowing the department head to recoup his

---

[1]The question of optimal mixed strategies in the game theory sense will not be explored in this thesis.

confidence so that management can again reduce the budget at a high rate. However, dc/dt can never be less for any department head at any time than the lower of the two rates shown in (2.6.28) and (2.6.29). It is therefore impossible to reduce cost, even instantaneously, at a rate which is greater than the optimum rate obtainable with a constant rate of budget reduction.

It is conceivable, however, that a greater amount of stress than M (say M') could be sustained for short periods while still maintaining encouragement, and similar remarks apply to the case for a higher failure point, N'. It would be necessary to keep $(c - a)$ below M at least part of the time if the short-run assumption is to be maintained. Nevertheless, a change in cost during a time interval t_0 to t_1 divided by the time interval may be expressed as

$$(2.7.1) \qquad \frac{\Delta c}{t_1 - t_0} = \frac{1}{t_1 - t_0} \int_{t_0}^{t_1} \frac{dc}{dt}\, dt = \frac{-\alpha_1}{t_1 - t_0} \int_{t_0}^{t_1} (c - a)\, dt$$

The right hand side of the relation is immediately recognized as $-\alpha_1$ multiplied by the average stress during the interval. Hence, an increase in $\Delta c/t_1 - t_0$ below $(-\alpha_1 M)$ can only be accomplished through raising the average stress. It is commonly accepted (in psychology,[1] if not in business management) that short periods of extreme stress must be counterbalanced by relatively stress-free periods of longer duration if neurotic behavior is to be avoided. If this psychological proposition holds true in the budget situation, then short periods of extreme stress where $(c - a) > M$ are useful as a short run device, but in the long run cause a slower rate of cost reduction.

It may be of interest, at least in passing, to examine a system which oscillates among four states of existence. Management will be said to be *optimistic* if it applies a rate of budget reduction which is sufficiently large to force an encouraged department head into discouragement and *pessimistic* if it applies a rate which is sufficiently small to cause the department head to return to encouragement.

The starting point for the cycle is irrelevant, at least for purposes of theoretical analysis. Hence, for convenience, the analysis may be started with the department head encouraged but with management still applying the smaller, pessimistic rate which was required to restore his encouragement. Let it be assumed that after a time delay, σ_1, management will change its budget procedure to the higher optimistic rate of

---

[1]See, for example, Finger (37a), Liddell (37c), especially p. 396, and Rosenzweig (37d) especially p. 387.

reduction, K_A. If K_A is sufficiently large, the department head will become discouraged. Management will again change its tactics, and after a time delay σ_2, will apply the lower rate of reduction K_B, which should be sufficiently small so that the system will return to the starting point and the cycle will repeat.

The first cycle may cause some difficulty if the department head is initially discouraged, and the discouragement is extreme. In order to allow management to choose a pessimistic rate for the oscillatory system which is sufficiently small to return the department head to encouragement in the steady state oscillation, but which may not be small enough to encourage the department head initially if the initial stress is very large, a third rate K_C is introduced which can be used initially, but ignored after the first management decision to change the budget. Otherwise, the rate K_B can be applied initially without complication.

After the first cycle, the discrepancy at the start of the cycle will be M since the department head will have just become encouraged. For the encouragement $\rightarrow$ discouragement and discouragement $\rightarrow$ encouragement transitions, respectively, the budgeted rates of cost reduction K_A and K_B required to maintain the cycle are specified in the "management action" column of Table 2.1. The expressions for the discrepancy $c - a$ as a function of time are shown in Table 2.2, which follows. The derivations are a result of straightforward but tedious application of equations (2.5.6a), (2.5.6b), (2.6.9), and (2.6.16)[1]. The change in cost which occurs during a cycle is

$$(2.7.2) \qquad \Delta c = - \frac{\alpha_1 \gamma}{\beta + \alpha_1} [K_A(\tau_1 - \sigma_1) + K_B \sigma_1]$$
$$- \frac{\alpha_2 \gamma}{\beta + \alpha_2} [K_B(\tau_2 - \sigma_2) + K_A \sigma_2]$$

where τ_1 and τ_2, as shown in Table 2.2, are the amounts of time spent in the encouraged and discouraged states, respectively, and their sum is the cycle time. Since both the cycle times and the cost reduction during a cycle are independent of both the absolute level of costs and (after the first cycle) of initial conditions, the oscillatory system is equivalent in effectiveness to a system with a constant rate of cost reduction given by

$$(2.7.3) \qquad \frac{dc}{dt} = \frac{\Delta c}{\tau_1 + \tau_2}$$

---

[1]These derivations, as well as a rigorous proof of the inferiority of the oscillatory system to the steady state system as a cost minimization device, are contained in the author's earlier paper (75), pp. 26-42.

TABLE 2.2. DISCREPANCY $(c - a)$ AS A FUNCTION OF TIME IN A FOUR-STAGE OSCILLATORY SYSTEM

Department Head	Management	
	Optimistic $K_j = K_A$	Pessimistic $K_j = K_B$
Encouraged: $\alpha_i = \alpha_1$	$Me^{-(\beta+\alpha_1)t}$ $+ \dfrac{\gamma}{\beta+\alpha_1}[K_A + (K_B - K_A)e^{-(\beta+\alpha_1)(t_1-\sigma_1)}$ $- K_B e^{-(\beta+\alpha_1)\sigma_1}]$ $\sigma_1 \le t \le \tau_1$	$Me^{-(\beta+\alpha_1)t} + \dfrac{\gamma K_B}{\beta+\alpha_1}[1 - e^{-(\beta+\alpha_1)t}]$ $0 \le t \le \sigma_1$
Discouraged: $\alpha_i = \alpha_2$	$Me^{-(\beta+\alpha_2)t'} + \dfrac{\gamma K_A}{(\beta+\alpha_2)}[1 - e^{-(\beta+\alpha_2)t'}]$ $0 \le t' \le \sigma_2$ $\tau_1 \le t \le \tau_1 + \sigma_2$	$Me^{-(\beta+\alpha_2)(t'-\sigma_2)}$ $+ \dfrac{\gamma}{\beta+\alpha_2}[K_B + (K_A - K_B)e^{-(\beta+\alpha_2)(t'-\sigma_2)}$ $- K_A e^{-(\beta+\alpha_2)(t'-\sigma_2)}]$ $\sigma_2 \le t' \le \tau_2$ $\tau_1 + \sigma_2 \le t \le \tau_1 + \tau_2$

$$\tau_1 = \frac{1}{\beta+\alpha_1}\ln\left[\frac{\gamma K_B - (\beta+\alpha_1)M - \gamma(K_B - K_A)e^{-(\beta+\alpha_1)\sigma_1}}{\gamma K_A - (\beta+\alpha_1)M}\right],$$

$$\tau_2 = \frac{1}{\beta+\alpha_2}\ln\left[\frac{(\beta+\alpha_2)M - \gamma K_A + \gamma(K_A - K_B)e^{-(\beta+\alpha_2)\sigma_2}}{(\beta+\alpha_2)M - \gamma K_B}\right]$$

(Note: The arrows indicate the order of procedure from one stage to the next within a cycle. Time is measured with the start of the cycle assumed to be in the northeast corner.)

The admissibility criterion for the steady-state model may be replaced by

(2.7.4) $$\Delta c \leq 0$$

The existence of admissible solutions is assured. Both $\tau_1 - \sigma_1$ and $\tau_2 - \sigma_2$ are positive, but the former can be made as large as desired by allowing γK_A to approach $(\beta + \alpha_1)M$ while the latter can be made to approach as close to zero as desired by reducing K_B.[1]

2.8. A Technological Constraint

In the interest of emphasizing the motivational aspects of budget control and not unduly complicating the model, technological constraints have been ignored. A technological constraint can be readily imposed, however, by the alteration of equation (2.5.2), leaving the model otherwise unchanged. Assume that, for a given level of stress and state of encouragement, it becomes increasingly harder to reduce costs as c approaches an optimum value, $\hat{c}$.[2] This assumption can be comprehended in a relation of the form

(2.8.1) $$\frac{dc}{dt} = -\alpha_i(c - a)e^{-\delta/c-\hat{c}} \qquad \text{where } c = c(t)$$

and where c and $\hat{c}$ are defined at some output level for a given "technology."

Note that questions of discrepancy between budgeted, aspired, and actual outputs are not dealt with as explicitly related to the technological constraint; only the rate of cost change is directly affected.

The adjustment of the aspiration level, viz.

(2.5.1) $$\frac{da}{dt} = \beta(c - a) + \gamma\frac{db}{dt}$$

remains unchanged. Provided conditions analogous to those for admissible rest in the original model,[3]

---

[1]*Ibid.*, p. 34.

[2]Cf. Charnes and Cooper (12) who discuss, in addition, the adjustment of c for output rates.

[3]Given an initially encouraged department head, *or* a budget sufficiently high to cause encouragement, thus resolving initial conditions difficulties, followed by a shift to the budget shown in (2.8.2a). Similarly, if $c - a$ is initially negative, application of rates of budget reduction as constrained in (2.8.2) will clearly force $c - a$ to become positive or zero.

$$(2.8.2a) \qquad 0 \leq -\gamma \frac{db}{dt} \leq M(\beta + \alpha_1 e^{-\delta/c-\hat{c}}) \qquad \text{or, } \alpha_2 \geq 0$$

$$(2.8.2b) \qquad N(\beta + \alpha_2 e^{-\delta/c-\hat{c}}) \geq -\gamma \frac{db}{dt} > M(\beta + \alpha_2 e^{-\delta/c-\hat{c}})$$

are met, $0 \leq c - a \leq M$. If $c - a = 0$ and $\gamma \frac{db}{dt} = 0$ the system is at equilibrium. If $c - a \neq 0$, then $\frac{dc}{dt} < 0$ and $c \to c$. But

$$(2.8.3) \qquad \lim_{c \to \hat{c}} \frac{dc}{dt} = 0$$

Hence the revised model is stable with an equilibrium solution given by

$$(2.8.4) \qquad \alpha_i \gamma \frac{db}{dt} e^{-\delta/c-\hat{c}} = 0$$

which requires, if α_i, $\gamma > 0$, either a zero rate of budget reduction or $c = \hat{c}$. The optimum rates of budget reduction are revisions of equations (2.6.28) and (2.6.29), viz.

$$(2.8.5) \qquad \begin{aligned} \frac{db}{dt} &= -\frac{M(\beta + \alpha_1 e^{-\delta/c-\hat{c}})}{\gamma} \\[2mm] \frac{dc}{dt} &= -\alpha_1 M e^{-\delta/c-\hat{c}} \end{aligned}$$

unless discouragement is slight and $N > \frac{\alpha_1}{\alpha_2} M$, in which case

$$(2.8.6) \qquad \begin{aligned} \frac{db}{dt} &= -\frac{N(\beta + \alpha_2 e^{-\delta/c-\hat{c}})}{\gamma} \\[2mm] \frac{dc}{dt} &= -\alpha_2 N e^{-\delta/c-\hat{c}} \end{aligned}$$

The model may be considered as a linear model with a finite number of discontinuities by letting

$$(2.8.7) \qquad \omega_r = e^{-/c_r - \hat{c}} \qquad \text{where } c_r \leq c < c_r + \rho$$

which provides

$$(2.8.8) \qquad \begin{aligned} e^{-\delta/c_r - \hat{c} + \rho} &< \omega_r \leq e^{-\delta/c_r - \hat{c}} \\ \lim_{\rho \to 0} \omega_r &= e^{-\delta/c_r - \hat{c}} \end{aligned} \qquad \text{where } c_r \leq c < c_r + \rho$$

allowing management to apply the rate of budget reduction

$$(2.8.9) \qquad K_r = \frac{M(\beta \pm \alpha_1 \omega_r)}{\gamma} \qquad \text{or } K_r = \frac{N(\beta + \alpha_2 \omega_r)}{\gamma}$$

depending upon whether it is desired to approximate (2.8.4) or (2.8.5), which will produce a rate of cost reduction less than the optimal rate but may be made to approach it by increasing the frequency of decision.

2.9. Conclusions

To comprehend the more complex situations which are likely to be encountered in practice it would undoubtedly be necessary to complicate the model, and this would, in turn, vitiate the objective of simplicity and clarity which is a *sine qua non* of a theoretical formulation at this stage of scientific work in budget control and cost behavior. But simple as it is, the analysis here presented does present some highly plausible clarification. For instance, once the department head's goal-setting pattern has been established, a static budget will tend to produce stationary expected cost, subject only to random variation about an expected value, in a viable ongoing situation. It is evident, furthermore (and psychological considerations appear to be strong enough to warrant this conclusion), that management cannot choose a rate of budget reduction for a particular department independent of considerations of the motivation structure of the department's head. Although this would appear to be obvious, the emphasis in today's literature is on budgeted costs and their relation to technology and not on their relationship to the individual being budgeted.[1] As noted in Section 2.8, technological constraints are an additional factor which must be considered, but technology,[2] important though it may be, does not obviate the necessity of also considering in any measure motives in a budgetary system which ultimately depend on some real consensus for their implementation. It is paradoxical that those who criticize mechanistic approaches to accounting (e.g., the research which treats human beings as servo-

---

[1] E.g., Keller (40), p. 98, states that, "The setting of standards is the responsibility of the technical staffs of a plant such as industrial engineers, design engineers, and chemists," although he later concedes that the foreman must agree that the standard is "fair." The problem of what to do if agreement is lacking, or what proportion of standards should be made to come into the area of questionable "fairness," is not related to the motivations of the individual concerned.

[2] In the literature of theoretical economics such technological factors (in the form of a production function) are accorded preponderant importance. But it must be remembered that the economic theory of the firm is based on a highly simplified model of the firm's "human" structure which, in turn, is justified by the fact that this model is designed primarily for analyzing "market" or general economic behavior and not the behavior of agents within a single firm.

mechanisms[1]) fall into the trap of a mechanistic approach themselves when applying (or explaining) rules of thumb to the problems of budgetary control.

The mathematics used in this chapter (and the logic with which it is associated) has been directed primarily to laying bare (and clarifying) certain issues which, though sometimes recognized in practice, are often concealed — or go completely unattended — in the existing literature on budgeting.[2] Certain by-products have also been achieved which will be explored in various ways in the chapters that follow. Thus certain issues involved in the strategy of setting budgets have been uncovered and related to each other in a way which related certain major factors to one another. Thus the budgeted amounts of the person to be controlled have been related to his actual cost performance with the aspiration levels acting as an intervening variable. Moreover, possible interactions between aspiration levels and cost performance have been examined. Finally, the objectives of those who seek to influence cost performance have been brought into the analysis, via the budgetary variables, in a way which raises most issues of strategy relative to the objectives of central management and thereby brings to the fore certain questions which are germane to adequate performance of the controller's office, as that office is now conceived.[3]

It is obvious, for example, that blanket budget reductions which are common in government bureaus and similar cost-saving "drives" in large corporations on a plant-wide scale are of dubious merit. Furthermore, the treatment of all subordinates "impartially" when it comes to budget demands, which essentially means treating them equally, regardless of their motivation structure, appears not only irrational from the cost standpoint but from the standpoint of welfare of the subordinates as well. For example, if a man at middle management level is directed to cut his budget, he may be able to "push" one man whose discouragement point is high to the limit and by so doing avoid discouraging a few

---

[1]See, for example, Anthony (1), who (rightfully) states that, "Human control systems cannot be so easily or so precisely designed as mechanical or electrical ones." Although he rejects the servomechanical analogy, he can only offer in substitution such comments as, "The method of constructing costs for control purposes is governed by management policy."

[2]Cf. e.g., Heckert (34) or MacDonald (53). This literature is almost completely occupied with the mechanics of budgeting to the point where it has assumed an almost standard form of presentation and development.

[3]Particular reference is made to the "control," as distinct from the "service," function in the sense in which these two terms are used in the controllership literature.

others whose discouragement points are lower, thus preserving morale and reducing costs further than he could by behaving "impartially." More specifically, if management desires to behave consistently over time, it must choose a more modest rate of budget reduction for the man who is easily discouraged than for the man who appears perpetually enthusiastic. Given two men with the same discouragement point, management must avoid discouraging the man who "when he is bad, is horrid," whereas the man who "when he is bad, is still slightly good" and doesn't give up easily can be kept on the verge of resignation for best cost results.

The models explored in this chapter indicate that an increase in stress, up to a point, is desirable in the reduction of costs. The assumption that standard costs must be "attainable," which pervades the current budget literature, is based on the assumption that the people who operate under them must be satisfied if they are to turn out a reasonable but unexceptional performance. But under even the very simple assumptions of the models in this chapter, it is evident that this need not be the case. Under certain circumstances the cost expected to obtain by a department head must be above his aspirations in order to ensure that he will work diligently toward reducing costs. Insofar as budgets affect his aspirations this kind of behavior must be taken into account; references to "loose" and "tight" budgets, with blanket approvals of the latter and condemnation of the former, as is common in the literature,[1] are not an adequate basis for dealing with this problem. Pending an explicit quantitative characterization in particular circumstances, the equations used in the models of this chapter have at least established a provisional qualitative characterization which suggests, instead, that budgets should be set rather in a way which allows an affected department manager to achieve his aspirations part of the time. In conclusion we note that this opens a rather broad range of questions concerned with the value of accuracy and timeliness of accounting (as distinct from budgeting) reports in terms of both their immediate and ultimate consequences for cost behavior.

---

[1]Some authors entirely dodge this issue by favoring only "accurate" budgets, failing to make clear whether they are speaking of the budget as a planning instrument or a control instrument.

CHAPTER 3

Available Empirical Information

3.1. Introduction

If, as is sometimes said, "Control exists in the minds of men rather than the books of account," then the theoretical model of Chapter 2 helps to highlight and formalize the kinds of psychological concepts that need to be considered. Of course such formalisms, however logical or elegant, are not enough in and of themselves to justify a theory. An empirical foundation is greatly to be desired or, failing this, some kind of testing and validation is required. Apart from the study by Argyris (2), which does not really deal with the central problem of cost responses to budgetary control procedures, there is (unfortunately) no systematic accumulation of evidence where the desired empirical foundation can be readily secured.

Failing access to a broadly based and systematic series of studies of managerial behavior under different budgeting arrangements, the following seem to be the best immediate alternative sources of empirical information: (1) studies that have been made of worker reactions to various incentive pay schemes, and (2) psychological (laboratory) studies (e.g., in aspiration level theory) which are more or less germane to the topic of interest. After these topics have been discussed in the sections immediately following, attention may be turned to one other source of information and possible validation. This information will be reported in the form of a laboratory experiment designed explicitly for the purpose of testing salient aspects of the theory which has now been advanced.

3.2. Laboratory Experiments on the Level of Aspiration

In this area, work in the laboratory has concentrated on descriptions of the formation of goals, taking performance as the independent variable, rather than manipulating performance through the effect of aspirations and external goals. However, valuable supporting evidence for the postulates of the mathematical model regarding aspiration level formation is available.

Chapman and Volkmann (7) asked a group of 86 students in psychology classes what score they hoped to receive on a test of literary achievement in which scores could range from 17 (by a random choice of answers) to the maximum of 50 questions. The students were divided into four groups. Group A was given no additional instructions while Group B was told that an average score of 37.2 was obtained by a group of authors and literary critics, Group C the same score for a group of students in psychology, and Group D the same score for a group of "unselected WPA workers."

The average aspiration levels[1] chosen by the four groups were 26.95 ± 6.33, 23.09 ± 3.46, 31.09 ± 8.95, and 33.05 ± 8.57. These differences were significant in pairs at better than the 1 per cent level, except for the A and B difference and the C and D difference, in which the probabilities of significant difference were .962 and .767, respectively. Also of interest was the significant correlation ($.523 \pm .105$) between aspiration level and performance in Group A. The authors concluded that, "The level of aspiration estimated in advance of performance is estimated neither at random nor without reference to the ability to perform the task."[2] The authors interpreted the results as evidence of the influence of the social environment in goal formation. It seems unlikely, however, that a group of college students would *aspire* to (i.e., set a personal goal at) a score 4 points lower than that attained by "an unselected group of WPA workers," although it is conceivable that their performance estimate[3] might incorporate such indications of inferiority feelings, interpreted perhaps in terms of fear of a new task.

Although the data show differences caused by reference to social

---

[1]It should be noted that the definition of "aspiration level" is not wholly consistent among writers in the psychological literature. For instance, the definition used by Chapman and Volkmann is not consistent with that of Frank (33), in that the latter explicitly requires previous experience with the task and makes formal and explicit provision for this, whereas this is not the case in the study reported above. In fact Chapman and Volkmann believe that the definition of aspiration level should be enlarged to include all estimates of performance that might be offered by the subjects regardless of previous experience.

[2]Chapman and Volkmann (7), p. 283.

[3]Unfortunately, I have not found a completely satisfactory method of separating aspiration and performance estimates, either. A discussion of this problem appears in Chapter 4.

groups, they also indicate that the subjects did not aspire to group norms in the abstract. For instance, if strong conformity to group norms were to be predicted, then Group C should have had an aspiration level average of about 37 instead of 31, since this score, the only general clue given them, explicitly referred to "a group of students in psychology." Moreover, on this hypothesis this group should have had a smaller variance (regarded as a measure of heterogeneity) than any of the other groups; whereas, in fact, the variance of this group was larger than any of the other three. An alternate explanation of the findings might be the perception of the 37.2 figure by the subjects as an *external goal* rather than a norm of a group, and with reference to this goal a subject would set his aspirations according to his perceived relationship to the group. But, of course, even this hypothesis is not fully satisfactory unless buttressed by further explanations such as the fact that the students were accustomed to aspiring to (or more likely predicting) performance below an externally imposed goal, while the amount of goal mitigation which took place was significantly affected by the reference to social groups. This conclusion would provide evidence for the validity of postulate (i) of the mathematical model; i.e., that the aspiration level is not necessarily set equal to the external goal, but is affected by it.

A second experiment of Chapman and Volkmann (7) was designed to assess the effect on level of aspiration of the achievements of other groups in a situation where they possessed prior knowledge of their performance. Four forms of 32 items each, taken from the Otis Self-Administering Tests of Mental Ability, were administered to the subjects on four consecutive days. On the second day the score on the first day's test was presented to the subjects and their aspiration level attained before beginning the second test. On the third day, the subjects were split into two groups matched in performance on the second day's test. Each subject in Group A was given the previous two days' scores and a third number (which was actually the average of his own test scores amended by $\pm.9$ to camouflage it) which he was told was the average score attained by a group of "unselected WPA workers," while a Group B subject was given the same information for "New York members of the National Academy of Sciences;" all subjects were given their scores and aspiration levels were ascertained. On the fourth day, each subject in Group A was told his score of the previous day as well as, "The average score of the class to date is 5.2 points below your average score to date."[1] The same information was also supplied to Group B except

---

[1] (7), p. 235.

that each of these persons was told that the average class score was 5.2 points "above" his average score to date.

The test results then gave estimated probabilities of a true difference between the mean aspiration levels of the two groups on the second, third, and fourth days as, respectively, .516, .655, and .520. The authors concluded that, "Under the conditions of this experiment, which included prior performance and knowledge of this performance, the level of aspiration was not changed by knowledge of the achievements of other groups."[1] These results would seem to indicate that in budgetary practice, the aspiration levels formed relative to similar budgets in several departments might be considered independently, particularly if the "my department is unique" attitude were initially prevalent. On the other hand, the experiment casts serious doubt on the possibility of affecting the aspirations of one department head by pointing out the achievements of another.

Other experimenters have concentrated on the generalization of expectancy along need-related lines.[2] Crandall[3] gave subjects two sets of stories similar to the Thematic Aperception Test. The experimental group was given a motor coordination task between the two sets, and told they did badly. It was found that the second set of tests showed lower "freedom of movement,"[4] relative to a control group which rested between sets of stories, in the areas of physical skill, academic skill, and love and affection of opposite sex peers. The differences between the groups were reported as significant at the 1, 2, and 20 per cent levels, respectively. The size and gradient of the decrements in freedom of movement (expectancy) were interpreted as indicating that the failure in motor coordination was generalized to need-related areas to an extent that was dictated by the closeness of the area to the need for recognition of the skill in which the failure experience occurred. If the results were to be taken at face value, the implications for budget control would be

---

[1]*Ibid.*

[2]The remarks offered on these experiments are based entirely on the work reported in Rotter (67). A good deal of additional work has also been done in the form of a series of Ph.D. dissertations at Ohio State University by S. J. Dean, R. L. Dunlap, A. A. Lasko, and D. E. Hunt. Unfortunately, however, I have yet to secure access to these additional documents, so the comments in this section rest entirely on Professor Rotter's reports including his summaries of the results secured by Drs. Chance, Crandall, and Jessor.

[3](22) cited in Rotter (67), pp. 120-122.

[4]Generally speaking, a measure of expectancy. In essence, the expectancy or performance estimate in an area appears to be correlated with the "abandon" with which a subject deals with that area. See (67), p. 110.

that no standard or budget for an individual could be set without reference to all of the others, since the need for recognition of skills required for budget attainment could not be expected to vary substantially from one budget to another. This need-relatedness would require, in addition to the difficulties of programming to determine the desired performance in each cost or performance subgroup, additional programming to take into account the effects of success or failure in achieving one budget on expectancy (aspiration) of another, as well as the main effect. However, as Rotter points out, "The results of this study could be explained by other theoretical approaches or as a function of uncontrolled similar factors in the experimental design."[1]

In an experiment of R. Jessor,[2] subjects were asked their expectations and minimum goals with regard to their performance on tests of (1) arithmetic, (2) vocabulary, (3) motor skill, and (4) social skill on which the average score was 25, ranging from 0-50. After the subjects were given an arithmetic test, they were told that their scores were a predetermined amount either below or above their minimum goal on that test. They were then asked to re-estimate their scores for another form of the arithmetic test and, since they had not taken the other three tests yet, allowed to change their estimates on the other three tests. The results were reported in terms of the proportion of subjects changing expectancies and minimum goals. Approximately 90 per cent of the subjects changed expectancies on the arithmetic task, 45 per cent on the vocabulary task, 35 per cent on the motor skill task, and 30 per cent on the social skill task. The proportions changing minimum goals were lower, but followed a similar gradient; approximately 65, 35, 25, and 20 per cent for the same four tasks. The gradients indicated were predicted by the experimenter on the basis of the amount of similarity of need or reinforcement based on a priori estimates of the similarity. It is my impression (borne out by experience with the experiment to be described in Chapter 4) that the ego-involvement of subjects in laboratory experiments, particularly those conducted in a classroom situation, is frequently exaggerated. The change of expectancies of Jessor's subjects could have been merely a result of the subjects "testing the test." Having the ability to utilize common sense along with the experimenter, a subject might feel that the information which he derived from his experience on the first test would be highly relevant to his estimation of the difficulty of a similar test. He may perceive the information he

---

[1]*Ibid.*, p. 121.

[2](39), in Rotter (67), pp. 121-124, 169, 191, 214, 215, 326.

possesses to be relevant to assessing a paper test of verbal ability, but unlikely to aid him in determining the scoring system to be used in a five-minute interview with a female member of the staff (test of social skill).

It would appear that the four tasks also follow a gradient in terms of testability; it is likely that this gradient would be perceived by the subjects. Furthermore, the gradient follows an introspective notion of the probable willingness of the subjects to change expectancies and minimum goals, in terms of the degree of relationship perceived by the subjects between the task and the *Gestalt*. I would predict, on this basis, that if the subjects in fact accepted the test score as a measure of their abilities, performance of the experiment in reverse (with the social skill task used as the reference point) would produce a considerably reduced gradient. On the other hand, the hypothesis that expectancy generalization is based on similarity of need would necessarily lead to a prediction of a new gradient very similar to the original. The changes in minimum goals could be interpreted as following directly from the changes of expectancy in order to (1) avoid the logical inconsistency of a minimum goal greater than the expectation and/or (2) maintain a more or less consistent difference between the expectancy and minimum goal perceived by the subject as "proper." Thus the experiment does show generalization of expectancy, but it falls short of demonstrating the dependence of generalization upon similarity of need.

A third study, which was designed to eliminate some of the physical stimulus generalization of the studies of Crandall and Jessor, was performed by Chance.[1] The tests were the same for the four experimental groups and of an unstructured nature based on more or less standard versions of ink blot and word associations tests. The four groups were told, respectively, that (1) both tests measured heterosexual adjustment, (2) both tests measured leadership potential, (3) the first test measured leadership potential and the second heterosexual adjustment, and (4) the first test measured heterosexual adjustment and the second leadership potential. The subjects stated expectancies for both tasks, performed the ink blot test and were given predetermined scores of either 7 or 14 points above their expectancies on the first task, and then were asked to restate their expectancies, which they could change if they wished. To quote Dr. Chance, she found that, "When the two tasks were described as need-related, there was significantly greater generalization than when they were described as measuring different skills."[2] Unfortunately the ex-

---

[1]Chance (6) cited in Rotter (67), pp. 124-125.
[2]Rotter (67), p. 124.

periment as it is described need not show anything about need similarity, but shows rather that subjects are likely to think that two tests measuring the same skill are likely to have the same scores. Perhaps the more important conclusion of the experiment is the indication that the 14-point increase resulted in significantly greater "generalization" than the 7-point increase; it would tend to indicate that the subjects have some intuitive notion of the concept of "significant difference" and the 7-point difference was not sufficiently far from the original value to merit changing the expectancy.[1] Either a 7- or a 14-point difference might seem insufficient motivation for inducing search behavior in some subjects but sufficient in others.

A possible lacuna in the three experiments, as reported, is that the results did not include the possibility that the change in expectancy was a result of the subjects' re-evaluation of the tests relative to their self-conception (which remained unchanged) rather than as a result of re-evaluation of themselves in terms of the tests. It is certainly conceivable that the adjustive reactions to even repeated failures on examinations for a population of students might, with some exceptions, tend to be extrapunitive.[2] That is, their covert (and possibly overt) behavior might tend towards re-evaluation of the test, the difficulty of the course, the fairness of the instructor, and the merit of the institution, at least for some period prior to undertaking an initial introspective appraisal. If these observations are true then some cloud may be cast on a series of studies which presuppose, by assumption only, that a subject's self-conception is changed radically during the course of an experiment involving one or two test successes or failures.

An aspiration level experiment which attempted to increase ego involvement by taking the subjects at least partially out of the laboratory was conducted by Siegel (70). A class of students in statistics agreed to accept a semester grade on the basis of an interview with an experimenter other than the professor. The professor was to return in an hour to discuss a student's grade if he were dissatisfied. All students were given the grade of C.

The students who wished to discuss their grades, by and large, were

---

[1] A hypothesis of Simon might be recalled here—viz., that a search for a new goal will not be instituted unless the original goal becomes unsatisfactory. See Charnes and Cooper (10), and see Chapter 2, p. 21.

[2] See (37d) for a more complete definition of this term; generally speaking, it is intended to describe cases in which an individual aggressively attributes his frustration or failure to external persons or causes rather than to deficiencies arising from his own being or behavior.

those who would have received an A or B in the course by the normal grading scheme.[1] Siegel concluded that the ones who returned did so because their aspiration level exceeded their grade. However, the grade has intrinsic *reward* value in addition to its more obvious function as a measure of achievement. It is not only that a student who *aspired* to an A received a C (he may have *expected* an A, in which case his ability to estimate his abilities was in question; or he may have thought he *deserved*[2] an A which involves principles of fairness, reward for hard work, etc.). Whatever its other merits, however, the Siegel experiment does not give results which could be an aid in the topics with which this book is concerned, except possibly to underscore the need for carefully defining pertinent characteristics of the variable under consideration.

A rather complete survey of the field of aspiration level experimentation up to 1944 has been performed by Lewin, Dembo, Festinger, and Sears (37b), which, with the exception of the first Chapman and Volkmann experiment, contains empirical studies which have not been treated here. The experiments they discuss have generally dealt with the precise interpretation of "level of aspiration" in various contexts and causal factors in shifts of the aspiration level. The causal factors investigated include social and personality factors as well as temporary situational factors. The theoretical model which these authors present to "clarify a situation which is at present a bit chaotic and to give orientation to further experimentation"[3] has been discussed in Chapter 2. In view of the situational dependence apparent in these studies, and the general lack of attempts to assess the possibility of influencing the behavior of the subjects through the aspiration level, nothing but their most general conclusions are possibly applicable to the problems of budget control as defined in this thesis. Since these general conclusions have already been stated (during the course of discussing other experiments), there is little point in singling them out for further separate treatment.

3.3. Experiments on the Behavior of Animals

A great deal of experimental psychology has been devoted to studying the behavior of animals. The advantages and limitations of this ap-

---

[1]There were some few exceptions to this statement. But these cases could have been predicted by previous experience with these individuals.

[2]E.g., via experience with past class norms, knowledge of course performance by his fellow students, etc.

[3](37b), p. 356.

proach are well-known, with the latter being particularly acute in any study of budgeting applied to managerial behavior. Nevertheless, in the interest of more complete documentation it may be well to make a few summary references to these results.

A case in point is the study of Birch (4). He tested six young chimpanzees and found that they performed best in three substantially different types of problems after a food deprivation of 6 hours, with food as the reward for a correct solution. The two food deprivations involving lower motivation (2 hours and 12 hours)[1] produced substantially poorer results, although the effect was more marked in those problems for which time of solution was the important variable. Among the more highly motivated circumstances, the 24-hour deprivation caused only slightly poorer behavior than the 6-hour trials, while the 36- and 48-hour deprivations produced markedly poorer performance. The percentage of "insightful" solutions to a hooked rope problem and 10 problems in the use of sticks was greatest for the 24-hour deprivation, and in descending order, 12, 6, 36, 2, 48.

Although the sample is too small to be reliable for this variable, it is interesting to note that the satisfied chimpanzees did not perform more insightfully when they had ample time to think about their problems. On the contrary, the best performance from the standpoint of *insight* appeared at a food deprivation (stress) somewhat greater than that of the best level of effective performance. In the 36- and 48-hour trials stereotypy was common and, for what it may be worth, the overall results quite consistent with postulates (iiia) and (iiib) of the mathematical model in the preceding chapter.

Another aspect of behavior which may be of relevance to budgetary practice is the motivating effect of fear. This aspect has been extensively investigated by Miller (78a) in a series of experiments on rats. Of particular interest is one in which learning behavior was tested after the initial pain stimulus had disappeared.

Each rat was given 20 shock trials, mixed with a larger number of nonshock trials, in one compartment of a two-compartment box. The rats quickly learned that they could escape through an open door into the second compartment. When placed into the same compartment *without* shock but with the door closed, the rats learned to open the door by pressing a lever. The maximum speed of door opening was attained by the rats between 5 and 9 days after the shocks ceased; a period which involved 100–180 nonshock trials. After a period of 30 days (360 non-

---

[1]The 12-hour is pre-breakfast whereas the 6-hour deprivation is a missed dinner.

shock trials) some of the rats were still pressing the lever to "escape" from the compartment in which the danger of shock had been long nonexistent.

Miller states that, "We may venture the hypothesis that learned anticipatory drive-reducing responses of fear obscure the true rate of drive in smoothly functioning human behavior."[1] If this hypothesis were to be substantiated, the effect of fear of dismissal or fear of demotion might produce (assuming the current state of knowledge) unpredictable responses to the budget control mechanism. Though beyond the scope of this paper, it is reasonable to assume that these unpredictable responses are likely to run counter to organization goals, and hence investigation of their effects would seem advisable in future research.

Still a third factor which would relate to the rewards associated with budget attainment has been investigated by Wolfe (85) who tested the effect of delay in reward on the performance of chimpanzees. He found that a group that, immediately following a work task, was given tokens with which to buy food at the end of a delay period was more willing to work than a group that performed the work task and merely waited for the food. The first group could tolerate a longer delay than the second, but when the delay became sufficiently long, the group could not be induced to work for the token.

He also tested the effect of the "capital stock" on the willingness to work. The chimpanzees were allowed to work for ten minutes to "earn" tokens with which to buy food. When they had no tokens at the beginning of a trial they earned an average of 21.2 tokens. When given 5, 15, and 30 tokens at the beginning of a trial, they only worked hard enough to earn an average of 15.2, 4.2, and 2.6 tokens, respectively.

Wolfe's experiments indicate that the amount of reward is not the only factor which influences performance. On the contrary, the timing of reward, the way it is administered, and the amount of reward on hand prior to the performance are factors which must be considered.

3.4. Studies of Utility Measurement

Another field which might be pertinent is the area of work which is concerned with empirical investigations in the measurement of individual utilities. This field is of interest at least insofar as it casts light on the problem of influencing behavior by means of monetary reward. For this reason some results of experiments in utility measurement will be presented.

---

[1]Miller (78a), p. 451.

Davidson, Suppes, and Siegel (24) performed gambling experiments with 19 subjects. The subjects were asked to choose between two alternative gambles, each of which had a small positive or negative payoff depending upon the throw of a die. From these experiments they concluded that:[1]

1. Under controlled conditions, some people (15 out of 19 subjects in the present experiment) make choices among risky alternatives as if they were attempting to maximize expected utility even when they do not make choices in accord with actuarial values.

2. For such people it is possible to construct a utility curve unique up to a linear transformation . . .[2]

3. Of the 15 subjects whose utility curves were determined, 12 had curves which were not linear in money.

4. Some evidence was obtained for the secular stability of subjects' utility curves . . .

Mosteller and Nogee (63) computed utilities of money (in small amounts), using 15 subjects in a gambling situation. In the basic game, the subjects were allowed to choose whether or not they wished to bet 5 cents on beating a particular "hand" in poker-dice. There were seven hands whose odds were such that a "fair offer" varied from 2½ cents to 5 dollars against 5 cents. The utilities, expressed as a multiple of 5 cents, were computed in terms of the bet which the subject was willing to make 50 per cent of the time (interpolating where necessary). Thus if a subject were indifferent to risking 5 cents to win 35 cents on a bet whose odds were 10:1 (fair offer = 50 cents), his utility of 35 cents would be 10 utiles. The subjects were given information as to what was a "fair offer" for each hand before the trials which were used for computation of utilities, and hence were aware of the objective probabilities and thus might have maximized expected return, *had they assumed the experimenter was benevolent.* It is, perhaps, not surprising that they did not attempt to do so. Three groups of subjects, run in groups of five, indicated considerably more similarity of utility within groups than between groups. Harvard graduates comprised two groups, while low income National Guardsmen comprised the third group. The Harvard students appeared to have a definite decreasing utility of money — but is it possible that they really wished to appear "conservative" before their fellow stu-

---

[1](24), p. 80-81.

[2]As required by the von Neumann-Morgenstern axiomatization of cardinal utility.

dents?[1] The Guardsmen, on the other hand, appeared to have increasing utility of money, but this could be explained purely in terms of gambling. Anyone experienced in games of chance is aware of the importance of being "a sport," and the Guardsmen, probably more experienced and having a higher utility of gambling per se, may very likely have vied with one another for their willingness to take risks since it was relatively inexpensive. Thus, the utility measurements of this experiment are very difficult to relate to a nongambling situation.

In addition to the problem of the utility of gambling, W. Edwards (30) has shown that subjects have a particular preference for certain probabilities. Furthermore, he found that subjects tend to exhibit greater preference for "long shots" when they are actually playing for money than when they were playing for worthless chips or "just imagining." Perhaps the most valuable piece of information that can be gleaned from the gambling literature, applicable to budget control, is the following, which is derived from observations on subjects who were forced to choose among bets whose expected value was negative ($-52\frac{1}{2}$ cents for all). As Edwards states,[2]

> The dominant fact about NEV [negative expected value] bets is that S's don't like to lose — they rather consistently prefer the alternative which had the lower probabilities of losing (and of course the higher amount of loss). This trend is so strong . . . that it obscures the other relationships which may be present.

If this result could be extrapolated with confidence to a typical budget situation, say the case of a department head who has several budgets to "make," then assuming that the penalty for missing each is the same, a rather interesting conclusion would emerge. The department head would, on this hypothesis, choose a course of action which would reduce the likelihood of "missing" on any budget instead of making all but one "safe" at the expense of the last. Such information would be extremely valuable as a basis for rational budgeting even after allowances were made for the fact that only an "average" or "representative" department head might behave in this manner.

---

[1]Two subjects in one group refused to bet more than 50 per cent of the time on an offer of 10 dollars where a fair offer was 5 dollars. The authors indicate that "for some subjects, the amount of money required to induce play against a hand may be so large that a project such as this one cannot afford the information." ((63) p. 382.) Since they stopped at an offer whose expected value was 10 cents, which would hardly seem exorbitant, it is probable that the authors were thinking in terms of absolute rather than expected value.

[2](30), p. 359.

Unfortunately, the case is not so clear either in logic or in evidence. J. Dreze (27) has presented a model designed to allow any decision situation to be described in terms of complex games. He indicates, however, referring to the experiments noted above and others utilizing similar monetary amounts, that "It seems highly dubious that observations about such trivial decisions could by extrapolation throw any light on the behavior of similar persons when faced with truly important problems."[1]

However, even the case for rationality is not uniformly accepted, as the following quotations show. For instance, Professor J. Marschak argues persuasively for the usefulness of rationality as a basis for analyzing industrial decision-making along the following lines:[2]

> At this point we can only hint at what is probably the most important virtue of the advice to maximize expected utility and, hence of the behavior postulates implied in this advice. We conjecture that, for a large class of distribution functions and utility functions, the following proposition is true: if every action is chosen in such a way as to maximize the expected utility, then, as the number of such actions is increased, the probability that the achieved utility differs from the maximum utility by an arbitrarily small number, approaches unity.

On the other hand, W. Edwards has presented a rather convincing opposing view. He first notes that:[3]

> The crucial fact about economic man is that he is rational. This means two things: He can weakly order the states into which he can get, and makes his choices so as to maximize something.

and, in later discussion:[4]

> There has, incidentally, been almost no discussion of the possibility that the two parts of the concept of rationality might conflict. It is conceivable, for example, that it might be costly in effort (and therefore in negative utility) to maintain a weakly ordered preference field. Under such conditions would it be rational to have such a field?

A recent study of business decision-making conducted by Cyert, Dill, and March (23) presents some evidence for questioning the concept of ubiquitous rationality in the behavior of businessmen. The question

---

[1]Dreze (27), p. 48.
[2](59), p. 139.
[3](31), p. 381.
[4]*Ibid.*, p. 382.

of whether or not business should behave rationally — and if so, where rational behavior might be "rationally" justified — is discussed elsewhere in this thesis. For the sake of concreteness this discussion is focused on specific types of decisions. However, in the context of attempting to assess the aspects of human behavior which would be useful in determining the reaction to budgets under various reinforcement schemes, the assumption of rationality on the part of the one who is to be controlled would probably lead to erroneous conclusions; i.e., although budgets are to be set so as to optimize performance, it is not believed that department heads will maximize monetary gain in an incentive system or have the weakly-ordered preference field required for rationality. Hence the results of the experiments discussed here may be relevant, but with serious limitations.

3.5. Some Field Studies and a "Practical" Example

The studies at the Hawthorne plant of the Western Electric Company are classic in the field of industrial psychology.[1] Among other things, "The experiments served an important purpose in calling attention to the fact that *interpersonal relations* and the character of the *social situation* can alter the effects of such [rest pauses and wages] specific incentives."[2] The evidence which is perhaps most important here, however, is the indication that change per se appears to be a factor in the output increase in the selected group of Hawthorne workers. Furthermore, there is no indication that the workers reacted unfavorably either to the increase in their hourly effort expenditure or to the emphasis on productivity (in terms of the incentive system and unaccustomed frequency of output measurements). If the Hawthorne results could be extrapolated to nonproduction workers, then they would clearly imply that changes in social factors might be employed to mitigate the dissatisfaction resulting from the expenditure of additional effort to improve performance.

A study whose findings are contrary to the usual assumption that people work better under permissive than under restrictive management is also of interest here. This study, which is nearly unique (among the studies reported here) in that it observed someone other than production workers, was performed by Wechsler, Kahane, and Tannenbaum (84).

The subjects were two divisions of employees including physicists, engineers, scientific aides, and supporting clerical personnel, designated

---

[1]For a summary, see (82), pp. 181-193, 214-215.

[2]*Ibid.*, p. 193.

as Division A and Division B. The head of Division A, containing 28 people, was a young brilliant scientist whose leadership was *restrictive;* Division B, containing 38 people, was headed by a less ambitious older man who exercised *permissive* leadership. Employee questionnaires indicated a considerably higher morale level in Division B. Although about 57 per cent of the employees of both divisions considered the productivity of their *work group* (a subgroup of a division) "high" or "very high" and only 3.6 per cent of Division A and 5.2 per cent of Division B considered the productivity "low" or very "low." The corresponding estimates of over-all Division B productivity by its employees were 55.2 per cent and 7.9 per cent, but for Division A 28.6 per cent and 18.6 per cent. The employees of the *permissive* Division B considered the productivity of the laboratory (consisting of several divisions) above average in 26.3 per cent of the cases, below average in 13.2 per cent; whereas the corresponding percentages in the *restrictive* Division A were 7.1 per cent and 32.1 per cent, respectively. Interviews were held with five superiors and two staff members who were familiar with the objectives and performance of the two divisions. The superiors rated Department A, in spite of its *restrictive* leadership, higher than Department B and higher than their own estimate of their performance.

It appeared that the director of Division A set objectives for his division which were more or less identical with those of his superiors, and in spite of low morale and low job satisfaction was able to "lead" his group into fulfillment of these goals. However, the director of Division B "utilized the services of a high morale group and of satisfied people in the performance of tasks which his superiors did not consider of highest importance to the laboratory."[1]

The study did not make clear precisely how much original research was conducted in the two groups or whether the *restrictive* leadership was equally binding on all members of Division A. It is also possible that more original work was produced in Division B while the objectives of the superiors may have been more short-sighted, reflecting an interest in problems of temporal rather than lasting interest.

Despite the ambiguities in this study, however, and despite the difficulty which surrounds the assessment of a proxy objective (and output) for a laboratory, it is interesting to observe that the low morale group was the high production group in this study.[2] There exists a strong

---

[1](84), p. 6.

[2]Confirmed also by University of Michigan studies of worker morale and productivity.

indication, furthermore, that the low job satisfaction might be attributed to stress caused by a higher level of aspiration in Division A, since it is reasonable to assume that the estimates of group productivity were set with reference to a "norm" which would constitute a level of aspiration for the division.

A practical example will be introduced to provide some evidence for the proposition that, whereas economics *assumes* an optimum production function, this is not likely to be the case in practice. Statistics compiled by the Lincoln Electric Company on their operations, for example, indicate a consistent reduction of cost and direct labor per unit output over time, both in absolute terms and relative to other producers of the same product.[1] These data cannot be explained entirely in terms of economies or diseconomies of scale (since the firm has been both small and large relative to the other firms in the industry), nor entirely in terms of technological change (since either new technology or at least the opportunity to acquire it would appear to be shared by the industry as a whole). Alternate hypotheses might be (1) that the production function, relative to a given technology, may depend on factors (e.g., psychological) other than those usually considered in economics and/or (2) that some or all firms in an industry do not operate at an optimum.

In the case of Lincoln Electric, many incentive techniques have been used which would not ordinarily motivate "economic man;" e.g., providing the workers with a sense of participation in management of the firm. In addition, an assumption which pervades Lincoln's approach (and is not altogether divorced from some of the assumptions which are made in the previous chapter) is the omnipresent possibility of improvement which may imply the existence of an optimum, but is incompatible with an assumption of current operation at an optimum.

The foregoing would serve to provide some validation to the investigation of control mechanisms as devices which influence the approach to optimality, although the evidence provided by such "practical examples" is necessarily vague and inconclusive. Further evidence for the non-optimal behavior of business firms is available from the study of Cyert, Dill, and March (23).

A convincing theoretical treatment which concentrates on the

---

[1]See (51) or (50). It should be noted that these data are company data and subject to obvious bias as such. However, the fact that Lincoln has lowered its price from $0.17 to $0.05 per pound for electrode and has, in the process, become the largest producer of that commodity, offers some supporting evidence for the above comments. Furthermore, these data have not, to my knowledge, been challenged by competing firms.

approach to optimality, rather than the a priori assumption of optimality, is presented by Charnes and Cooper (11). The approach they use embodies a more structured definition of the cost structure than is used here, and hence is of great interest in implementing the more explicit statements of the psychological factors in this paper.

3.6. Conclusion

The studies presented in this chapter provide a cross section of the evidence available about human behavior which might be applicable to an individual in a budget-controlled activity. More, of course, could be presented, but it is hoped that this brief survey will at least provide some background for the analyses and experiments which will be dealt with in the following chapters.

To summarize, there is evidence that individuals form either individual goals or estimates of their performance (or perhaps both). On the other hand, it is not precisely clear which of these is being formed at any given instant. These aspirations (or expectations) tend to be decreased following a failure in a previous trial in the same task, or increased by a success in that task. The aspirations are affected by external reference points other than performance, but this effect tends to decrease as experience with the task increases. (However, the effects of rewards have not been clearly determined.) The aspiration level is subject to change with success or failure on related tasks, but it is not clear whether the effects can be explained by stimulus generalization or by similarities of need.

Animal studies of motivation are a potential source of information, but the problems of inference relating them to human behavior are not solved even in general, so that use of information gleaned from these studies is of dubious value for the subject with which this thesis deals.

Experiments in utility maximization have used, as a basic premise, the "rationality" of man. On the one hand, these studies are by and large oriented only to an individual's tastes and performance. On the other hand, there is no universal agreement on the basic postulates. Furthermore, these experiments have been conducted with amounts of money whose expected values are, as Dreze notes, in danger of being regarded as trivial by the subjects. This further attenuates the results secured (since they become even more difficult of extrapolation to an actual situation) and, hence, tends to reduce the reliability of conclusions that might otherwise be drawn.

Field studies have shown conflicting results, and only isolated examples of studies which indicate the possibility of introducing an adequate control scheme appear. A further weakness (from the standpoint of this study) is that almost all of the more substantial studies in this area have been directed primarily towards the behavior (motives, etc.) of production workers, as distinct from budgeting or budgeted management.

Business experience, though voluminous, tends to be so loosely phrased (or reported) and to contain such a mixture of complex and unresolved factors, that little can be gained, at this time, by a recitation or analysis of this experience. It therefore has seemed best to confine the presentation here to a single instance where the management has at least been more articulate than most. It is interesting — although, of course, not decisive — that this company (the Lincoln Electric Company) has issued its series of pronouncements in a form which is not wholly incompatible with the theory covered in the preceding chapter.

CHAPTER 4

An Experiment

4.1. Introduction

The brief survey of received evidence, analyses, and hypothesis (i.e., the survey just concluded) does not reveal any body of material which is sufficiently pointed either to validate or even to give satisfactory guidance for a theory of budgetary control of the kind which is of interest here. With this in view, an experiment was designed to see what could be uncovered by the laboratory techniques of experimental psychology when these are combined with the principles and tools of modern statistical inference, as exhibited by the theory of experimental design, and the tools provided by the analysis of variance, etc.

In the experiment which will now be reported, a major objective was to investigate relations that might exist between individual performance and aspiration levels and the relations that might also exist between these variables and the kind of "external"[1] goals which are represented by a budget of the kind commonly employed in management practice.

From one standpoint this experiment may be regarded as an attempt to repair existing gaps in the extant literature. In particular, it is designed to help remedy a situation where no satisfactory and explicit attempt has been made to ascertain the effects of varying aspiration level upon performance, and also to supply some modicum of evidence on the effects of explicit goals (e.g., those emanating from an experimenter)

---

[1] I.e., goals which are at least partly external in the case of any single individual where the term "external" allows the possibility of a group or other norm to which an individual may willingly (consciously or unconsciously) conform.

as they bear on either (or both) of the other two variables. From another standpoint the results of this experiment may (it is hoped) be regarded as a beginning towards the accumulation of a systematic body of evidence upon which an improved understanding of the problems of budgetary control may be built.

It is to be emphasized that the results of this one experiment do not warrant any firm conclusions on the problems of budgetary practice as they are found in actual management systems. Nevertheless, a beginning, if it is to be made somewhere, might as well start with the kinds of factors — external goals, aspirations, and performance — that are included in this experiment. In the present stage of knowledge, the advantages of a laboratory test appear to outweigh anything that might be gleaned from alternate approaches; e.g., a broad survey of existing industrial practice or intense studies of a few selected cases.[1]

The budgets used in the experiment are of a kind sometimes referred to as "performance budgets."[2] By this it is meant that the measures, hence the controls, are gaged with respect to physical quantities only. "Cost budgets" — i.e., budgets cast in terms of dollar amounts — are not covered.

It may be recalled at this point that the models and analyses of Chapter 2 were couched in terms of "cost behavior" rather than "physical performance" as such. Formally, the difference is easily attended to. For instance, a substitution of p (performance) for c (cost) in equations (2.5.1) and (2.5.2) accompanied by the use of $(a - p)$ rather than $(c - a)$ as a measure of stress associated with aspiration level discrepancies provides a restatement of the requisite kind. Correspondingly, the technological conditions would also be restated by replacing $(c - \hat{c})$ with $(\hat{p} - p)$ in the exponential. But of course, matters of formal equivalence do not necessarily establish or resolve empirical questions which involve actual (psychological) behavior responses. It is possible, for example,

---

[1] In any event such surveys and case studies have been made by others, and reports of results are available in the standard literature.

[2] This should not be confused with this same term as it appears in *The Hoover Commission Report on Organization of the Executive Branch of the Government* (36). Cf., e.g., p. 36, Recommendation No. 1, which proposes that, "The whole budgetary concept of the Federal Government should be refashioned by the adoption of a budget based upon functions, activities and projects: this we designate as a 'performance budget'." Also, further on, "Under performance budgeting, attention is centered on the function or activity — on the accomplishment of the purpose — instead of on lists of employees or authorizations of purchases . . . It places both accomplishment and cost in a clear light before the Congress and the public."

that budgets cast in terms of cost might have effects which differ from those couched in terms of physical (performance) measures only. It is also possible that budgets stated in both cost and physical terms may have still different consequences, since logical and psychological equivalences are not necessarily isomorphic.[1]

Bearing these kinds of considerations and qualifications in mind, the gist of the experiment actually undertaken will now be described.

4.2. The Experimental Task

Each subject took a series of 6 tests, each containing 15 water-jar problems of the type used by Luchins (52).[2] In each of these problems a subject is told that he has 3 empty jars of different capacities (expressed in integers). He must, without approximating, fill the jars from a tap and then empty them into a sink or into one another in such a way that he obtains a required (integral) number of quarts as the total amount of water in the jars at the end. A simple example will be more enlightening than a further explanation of the rules of the game. A 2-jar problem might be as follows: "You have a three-quart jar (A) and a two-quart jar (B), and you are required to obtain one quart." An appropriate solution would be: "Fill A, fill B from A, empty B," leaving the required one quart in A. A second solution would be "Fill B, fill A from B, fill B, fill A from B, empty A," leaving the required one quart in B. Either sequence of steps would be considered correct. It will be noted, of course, that either of these solutions can be expressed algebraically (viz. $A - B$ or $2B - A$), but the problems were "sugar-coated" in order to avoid possible antimathematical "blocs" associated with presenting them as problems in algebra.

The 6 tests, as constructed, were intended to be "equally" difficult. But, as the subsequent statistical analysis revealed, this objective was

---

[1]Thus, it is to be noted that the formal (mathematical) transformation introduced does not really come to grips with issues often discussed in the budgetary literature on such matters as to whether overhead and fixed elements of cost should be included in the budget or to whether each supervisor should be budgeted (hence held accountable) only for variable items of expense that he can directly control (rather than merely indirectly affect). Furthermore, the experiment does not really deal with "group endeavors," nor does it deal with issues such as "cost circulation" and related allocation issues. Some of these topics will be discussed later in this paper but without the benefit of experimental evidence — which it is hoped will be generated at a later time.

[2]A sample test and instructions given to the subjects are shown in Appendix 4A, pp. 96-102.

not wholly achieved. A general description of the choice of the tasks is as follows:[1] The capacities of the jars were chosen at random. The solutions (i.e., formulae expressed in terms of jar capacities which yield the required number of quarts) were chosen at random from subsets of possible solutions which were constant from test to test. In order to provide for a desired rough ordering of problems (in terms of difficulty), the subset from which problem 1 was chosen contained very simple solutions; whereas the subset for each subsequent problem was determined by eliminating some of the simpler solutions contained in the subset for the previous problem, while adding an equivalent number of more difficult solutions.

The selection process was intended to provide a gradual increase in the difficulty of the problems on any one test as the subject worked from beginning to end. As a result of various peculiarities in the problems (explained in detail in Appendix 4A), it would have been difficult, if not impossible, to determine an a priori measure of difficulty sufficient to provide a precise ordering, even if the overlapping of solution subsets were to have been eliminated. Examination of the experimental data indicated that, among other things, the ordering depended upon the particular skills of a subject. Uniqueness of the solutions could not be guaranteed nor, as will become evident in the following remarks, was it considered advisable to eliminate problems having a multiplicity of solutions. The measure of performance used was the number of problems correctly solved (independent of difficulty) in the seven-minute trial period allowed for each test.

With this much of the experimental background at hand and with some of the attendant difficulties now set forth, it may be helpful to examine these issues from the standpoint of similar problems as they might be expected to occur *in situ* in industrial practice. A simple illustration would be one involving a department head, a foreman, or other such individual in the echelons of "budgeted management." Let it be supposed that this individual is given a set of problems (or tasks) which involve some degree of intellectual application combined with judgment in varying degree; and let it be further supposed that (a) a set of standards is imposed and that these vary by some presumed order of difficulty, although (b) not all of the problems have a unique solution.

Note that the goals or other criteria incorporated in the varying

---

[1]A description of the selection process utilized in the determination of the task, sufficiently detailed to allow reproduction of the tasks used here (subject to random deviation), appears in Appendix 4A, pp. 93-95.

standards may not correspond to "real" orders of difficulty and, a fortiori, may not conform to the order of difficulty which a particular manager might either find apparent or else experience in actuality. Moreover, neither the standards nor the actual performance may meet the optimizing requirements of the economic theory of production — in which nonuniqueness is resolved by the assumption of optimization per se.[1]

As already noted, no claim is made that the results of this study are immediately ready for extrapolation and application to industrial practice. Nevertheless, the motivation of the study is such that the relevance of the theories, designs, etc. for general classes of problems, as they might be encountered in management practice, was constantly borne in mind, and the resulting experiments were judged, so far as possible, by reference to this kind of possibility. From this standpoint, and within the limits already noted, it is therefore interesting to note that the features of task selection which caused difficulty from a purely scientific standpoint are of the same kind that might be expected to prevail, at least under certain circumstances, in practice.

In the experimental setting (lacking an explicit formulation of cost or production as a function of problems solved), the measure of performance chosen was the number of problems per se. The time limit is in accord with the hypothesis implied in the model of Cooper and Charnes (11),

---

[1]The imposition of optimality conditions, as found in economic theory, provides a convenient way of reaching uniqueness. But actually this resolution is assumed, rather than proved (or empirically validated), in economic theory. Cf., e.g., A. Charnes and W. W. Cooper (11), or Sune Carlson (5), pp. 14-15: ". . . If we want the production function to give only one value for the output from a given service combination, the function must be so defined [sic] that it expresses the *maximum product* obtainable from the combination at the existing state of technical knowledge. Therefore, the purely *technical* [sic] maximization problem may be said to be solved by the very definition of our production function." Presumably Carlson, as a typical economist, means that someone else (e.g., engineers) solve this problem so that learning and other such adjustments are absent. But as R. Dorfman, P. A. Samuelson, and R. A. Solow (26) somewhat humorously note in *Linear Programming and Economic Analysis*, p. 131:

> The production function is a description of the technological conditions of production, and the economist takes no direct responsibility for ascertaining it. Instead he regards it as falling within the purview of the engineer. But there seems to be a misunderstanding somewhere because the technologists do not take responsibility for production functions either. They regard the production function as an economist's concept, and, as a matter of history, nearly all the production functions that have been derived are the work of economists rather than engineers.

where it is assumed, when learning and adjustment are allowed for, that a supervisor's ability to approach optimality in a particular phase of operation is limited by the amount of time he can devote to that phase. Likewise, the problems which occur in an industrial setting do not necessarily have a unique solution, and it is reasonable to assume that frequently problems are solved just as effectively (except for the additional time involved) by a roundabout method even though a simpler solution may exist.

From a statistical standpoint, the rough ordering introduced was utilized as a means for avoiding the possibility of extremely large differences in scores arising between subjects who proceed from easy to "more difficult" problems, in contrast to those subjects who might either proceed on an opposite course or else "plod straight through" the problems in the order given in a particular test. Such differences might easily produce bi-modal, tri-modal, or (in general) multi-modal distributions and thereby (a) obscure the main effects or (b) require recourse to complicated statistical analyses.

The reasons for introducing problems of varying difficulty may also need to be explained. First, despite the ranking difficulties already discussed, it is still harder to design a battery of "equally difficult" problems. A possible exception is, of course, the case where all problems in a test are exactly the same.[1] If this were an experiment in, say, rote learning, such an approach might have been adopted. Not only was this not the case, there were also difficulties that might be anticipated in view of the choice of experimental subjects (university students) who might react to the resulting ennui with complete diminution of effort. Second, there was some interest in ascertaining the effects on performance with variations in task difficulties. *Inter alia* it was desired to ascertain whether consistency of performance might be achieved via a learning route under which experience carried over from simpler problems was applied (later) to more complex ones.[2] Third, a range of available problems introduced a safety factor in the design which could be utilized if analyses — carried on *pari passu* with the tests — showed anything to be going seriously awry. For instance, a preliminary inventory of more difficult problems would be available in case the motivation (or

---

[1]But note that issues still arise in connection with repeated solutions of the same problem; e.g., discouragement associated with initial failure as well as the "jumps" which are likely to occur after a first success is achieved.

[2]It should be noted that, although the tests were of (approximately) equal difficulty, the "budgeted learning" was such that the subject was expected to do more (and hence more difficult) problems as he proceeded through the series of trials.

other) analyses showed any lack of interest or boredom on the part of a significant number of the subjects already examined.[1] Finally, the use of a range of more and less difficult problems made it possible to analyze these effects per se — and these effects are not uninteresting for the problems of practice — and also avoided the need for undertaking unnecessary extrapolations in this direction on the basis of a more limited range of evidence.

With this much of the reasoning now explained, it is desirable to turn to a discussion of other aspects of the experiment; namely, a problem involving not merely "intellectual" (e.g., learning) carryover, but also carryover of problems existing in the industrial setting. It was, in fact, found to be impossible to ascertain, even approximately (in the experimental setup), the effect of an inventory of *unsolved* problems which "carries over" from one period (or trial) to the next. Nor was it deemed desirable to complicate matters by utilizing an approach which introduces certain "crucial problems," which must be correctly solved as a precondition for receiving recognition for any performance at all. Such an approach, of course, has a certain appeal from the standpoint of its potential bearing on the problems of actual budgetary applications in management so that its omission is justified only by expediency and immediate practicality. It's omission from the list of experimental factors mentioned here may therefore be regarded as one more qualification relative to the problems of actual budgetary practice.

4.3. The Reward Structure and Budget

A "budget"[2] was set for each subject for each test. Before the start of the trials, each subject was given $3.00. If the subject "made his budget" (solved the budgeted number of problems or more) he was given an additional dollar. If he solved fewer problems than the budgeted number, he was required to pay the experimenter $1.00 from his pre-

---

[1]The problems which arise in the construction of equally difficult (but different) tasks for subjects in a situation in which learning is a factor are not trivial. Chapman, Kennedy, Newell, and Biel (8) found that a group of college students "learned its way right out of the experiment," enabling them to perform adequately while engaging in nontask activities while a trial was in progress. Based on this experience, succeeding trials in their experiment were designed to reflect the hypothesis that task difficulty was not determined by the number of problems per se but by the number of problems relative to the group's (learned) problem-solving capacity of the moment.

[2]For fear of possible misunderstanding, the term used with the subjects was "goal." Cf. Appendix 4A.

viously accumulated sum. Thus both positive and negative rewards were involved, and a potential difference of $2.00 in asset position was at stake in each single test of seven-minute duration.[1]

As already noted, each subject was given $3.00 at the start of the experiment. In order to avoid automatic failure via exhaustion of resources on the fifth or sixth test, each subject was allowed to make a dollar on either of these. In any event, no subject was required to deplete his own funds beyond the loss of the initial $3.00 plus accumulated earnings. In sum, any subject could theoretically leave the experiment having earned as much as $9.00, or as little as nothing.[2]

The subjects were divided into four groups of equal size and labelled A, B, C, and D according to the kind of budgetary situation for which they were to be tested. Group A represents what will be called an "implicit-budget" group. This group was never told what their budgeted amount on any test was to be. In contrast, Groups B, C, and D will be called the "explicit-budget" groups. Where explicit budgets were involved, subjects were informed of their budgets before each test trial.

In addition to the explicit-implicit classification, the budgets applicable to the four groups were further subdivided into a "low," "medium," and a "high budget." On the first test for all groups (implicit as well as explicit) the budget was set at 5 problems (correctly solved). In Group B, the "low budget" group, the budgets for the subsequent tests were obtained by adding alternately 1 and 0 to the previous test score. For Group C, the "medium budget" group, the "adjustment" was alternately 2 and 1; and for Group D, the "high budget" group, 3 and 2. Group A (implicit budgets) was further subdivided into three groups, each third having a budget determined in the same way as one of the "explicit budget" groups.

---

[1]The experiments of Mosteller and Nogee (63) used amounts whose expected value was at most $0.10. Davidson, Suppes, and Siegel (24) used amounts up to $0.50, but only rarely. Edwards (29) used prizes which ran as high as $6.00. (It is proposed in a subsequent experiment to ascertain the effects of variation in monetary rewards.)

[2]Actually, if the subject's stock of capital was less than $3.00 at the beginning of the sixth test, the grading (done away from view) was arranged so that the subject automatically "made the budget" regardless of his score or, if a subject's stock was $8.00, he automatically failed to make the budget on the last test. (The first few subjects, depending upon their stock of capital, were given an easy, normal, or difficult seventh test on which the reward or penalty was $2.00, but this increased the time considerably without supplying much additional information. In view of this a switch was made to the above procedure, which, as far as could be ascertained, worked satisfactorily.)

An issue which is often of interest, at least as far as the literature of budgeting and standard costing is concerned, deals with presumed advantages and disadvantages of optimal (or ideal) standards versus "tight-but-attainable standards" and budgets which are "too loose" or "too tight."[1] These statements are usually couched in loose and very general terms which, apparently, are intended to apply over a great variety of situations as well as to persons of differing socio-psychological makeups and needs.[2]

It is of interest in this connection to note that the "low budget" of the experiments is the only one that may be said to correspond to the often-cited principle of "attainable but not too loose."[3] In contrast, the principle of budgetary adjustment utilized would require, for the medium budget groups, successive attainments in the amount of 5, 7, 8, 10, 11, and 13 (or better) problems correctly solved as the trials proceeded.[4] These figures assume an additional constraint — viz., that a subject running through the indicated sequence of trials could do, at most, one additional problem on 2 tests or 2 problems on one test. (This allows for the rule for adjusting the succeeding budgets, relative to past performance, that was employed.) Finally, the "high budget" was mathematically incapable of attainment over all trials so that it lies at the opposite end of the spectrum.

A word also needs to be said about the implicit-budget category which was also (it will be recalled) subdivided into low, medium, and high for test purposes. In part, this group served the purpose of a statistical

---

[1]Cf., e.g., Walter B. McFarland (61) for a succinct summary. See also, R. M. Trueblood and W. W. Cooper in their article "Cost Accounting" in the *Encyclopædia Britannica* (79).

[2]See, e.g., Stanley B. Henrici (35), Chapter III ff. It is to be noted that Henrici, in common with many writers, is inclined to draw overly fine distinctions between "budgeted" and "standard" costs since, as he himself admits on p. 29, "As a matter of fact, both [i.e., budgeted costs and standard costs] may be used coordinately in the same enterprise. The difference [if any] lies in the use to which they are put . . . .."

[3]*Vide*, e.g., McFarland, *op. cit.*, p. 154: ". . . in the related field of time study . . . it seems generally agreed that a standard rate should be attainable by a majority of the workers." See also Henrici, *op. cit.*, p. 30: ". . . the only arguments against 'ideal' (i.e., optimum) standards is that they are difficult to sell . . . [It is important] that the supervisors will know that they have been set a task possible of achievement."

[4]Actually only one subject in the B classification attained the budget on every test, although 4 subjects in other groups had scores sufficiently high so that (assuming away budgetary- and aspiration-level effects) their performance would have clocked off the required minimal amounts in every trial of the B group.

control in order to handle confounding which might otherwise occur. But it is also of interest in its own right. The practice of implicit budgets is probably still widespread in industrial practice. In particular, even firms with developed budgetary practices do not necessarily have every item, every supervisor, and every operation necessarily encompassed in the formal budgeting procedures.[1] In fact, it is common, even in the literature, to distinguish between "complete" and "incomplete" budgets to accommodate these kinds of cases.[2]

It cannot be safely assumed, however, that merely because a systematized and formalized procedure is absent, supervisors not covered by an explicit budget do not then believe that others (e.g., their superiors) hold no expectations concerning their behavior. And, after all, the essence of the budgetary control procedures is formulated around such "external" expectations which become crystallized as a stated goal when formalized in either a budget, a physical or cost standard, etc.

To state the matter differently, it would have been possible to effect the indicated statistical resolution by introducing a "no budget" group for control purposes. This was not done, however, for the reasons already stated: It is difficult to conceive of a managed situation under which some one or more individuals (who are subordinate to others) would be given a completely free hand without any notion that others were at least informally forming goals or standards by which to judge their performance. It therefore seems logical to turn in this direction and to introduce the additional replicates involved — i.e., a low, medium, and high implicit budget — to satisfy the statistical requirements when this has been done.[3] It was then felt (or rather hypothesized) that the groups would attempt to infer from the resulting penalties or rewards what kinds of (implicit) budgetary levels were involved.

It is important now to detail the kind of information supplied to the subjects with respect to the budget-setting and accounting procedures.

---

[1]Cf. R. M. Trueblood and W. W. Cooper, *loc. cit.*

[2]Thus, E. L. Kohler (44) observes, on p. 67, under the term *budget:* "... Complete budgets covering all phases of an enterprise as well as incomplete budgets covering only certain phases are also met with in practice."

[3]If such replications are not introduced, it becomes necessary to have recourse to rather involved statistical formulas, many of which have to be worked up *de nouveau* since, apart from so-called missing lot-plot analyses (generally of an agricultural variety), the literature of statistics does not provide readily available formulas, but only general guides to the kinds of adjustments that would be needed — including adjustments for unequal subgroups, etc.

Here again it was desired to conform as closely as possible to situations that might be encountered in practice. In particular, it was desired to reproduce (in so far as this was possible) a situation in which the subjects know only general policies — often in a somewhat vague form — and have only a loose notion of their actual attainments as gleaned directly from their own experience. There is also a question of "informal" as well as "formal" policy to be dealt with. Thus an actual budgetary adjustment process may be utilized (as distinct from one which is formally stated) and the individual left to his own devices insofar as inferences about this process are concerned.

In the tests as run, the subjects were informed verbally that the goals were set "according to your individual performance." Subjects were not informed of their scores and the tests themselves were designed so that the subjects would not be likely to know their exact numerical scores — i.e., number of problems successfully solved. A posteriori, most subjects did not work straight through and few counted the number they had done; furthermore, the probability of error was high so that even an actual count would not suffice to give a firm answer on the number of problems *correctly* solved.[1]

The vagueness of information supplied to the subjects combined with the alternating adjustment appeared to be quite effective in camouflaging the budget setting process in all but a few cases. The main purpose of not revealing scores, however, was to reduce the amount of information the subject received to compensate for the direct correspondence between budgeted number of problems solved and budget performance.

Further discussion of this topic is now best delayed until the results of the statistical analyses can be presented.

4.4. Aspiration Level Determination

Attention will now be turned to the methods that were utilized for determining aspiration levels.

It will be recalled that the interest of the study for this factor extends to possible relationships between budgets, aspiration levels, and performance. For this purpose each of the four budget groups — A, B,

---

[1]The possibility of error would, of course, be expected to lead to a somewhat biased estimate of the score. Purely qualitative indications of this bias — viz., expressions of disappointment upon failure to receive reward — were received by the experimenter. No attempt was made to ascertain the effects of this bias on aspiration and/or performance.

C, and D — were further subdivided into three groups, α, β, and γ, according to the time precedence for securing aspiration levels and presenting budgetary information. In group α no aspiration level statements were called for. In Group β aspiration levels were stated in advance of any budgetary information, whereas in Group γ exactly the reverse information process was employed so that this group had the requisite budgetary information at hand before stating its aspiration levels.

A description of this part of the design may, perhaps, best commence with Group β — i.e., the group consisting of Aβ, Bβ, Cβ, and Dβ. Before each test, but after the rewards and penalties for the previous test had been distributed, each subject was asked "How many problems do you hope to complete on test X?"[1] To avoid, or at least to avoid reenforcing, a plausible (but untrue) inference that his aspiration level statement might be used in setting subsequent budgets, the following procedure was employed. Each β subject was instructed to turn the questionnaire face down before him as soon as he had answered the questions. He was told also that none of these questionnaires would be collected until all six tests had been completed. On the other hand, to eliminate the possibility of ex post facto adjustments of stated aspirations by reference to actual performance, the subject was not allowed to change any statement on a turned-over questionnaire or even to refer to it when completing subsequent questionnaires.[2]

Only after β had stated their aspiration levels was the budgetary information given to them for the next test. And only after all tests had been completed — each test being collected at the end of each trial —

---

[1]Certain additional questions, as exhibited in Appendix 4A, were also asked in a not wholly successful attempt to validate, or at least qualify, whether or not the received statement actually represented a "true" aspiration level. Also, it should probably be noted that rewards and penalties were simultaneously distributed among the subjects at the same time as the first piece of paper (questionnaire or budget) was distributed, during the interim periods which obtained between tests. On this first piece of paper the qualitative score (success or failure) was also noted for each subject: a(+) if he had attained the budget on his last trial and a(−) if he had not.

[2]Of course, in actual budgetary practice such aspiration levels may have exactly the indicated adjustment effect via the negotiation (and signature) processes that are often associated with budget setting. On the other hand the context of this experiment indicated that such effects might be highly unpredictable and possibly swamp, via variance increases, other aspects of the study which were more immediately interesting. The larger number of trials or resulting complications in the design and analyses necessary to overcome this possibility were not deemed to be warranted in terms of the choices that necessarily had to be made within the study limits.

were the questionnaires for this group collected.[1] (These questionnaires had, of course, been pre-coded for purposes of collation in the subsequent statistical analysis.)

For the γ group — i.e., Aγ, Bγ, Cγ, and Dγ — the rewards, penalties, qualitative scores, and budget information for the next trial were distributed at the same time as the questionnaire. Hence each γ knew his budget before being called upon to state his aspirations.

Finally, for Group α, no aspiration level statements were asked for. Here the subjects were given their rewards and penalties, the relevant budgetary information (as they fell into implicit or explicit budgetary groups) along with the tests for the next trial. This group could therefore immediately set to work, without being bothered to supply information on the intervening variable, "aspiration level."[2]

An attempt was made to find "minimum goals" for the subjects as well.[3] However, the question, "Do you believe that you should be penalized if you do not complete as many problems as you hope to?" was usually answered in the negative. Hence the answer to the third question was frequently nonexistent, and also some strange results (such as a minimum goal greater than the aspiration level) appeared. The questionnaire following the test gave indications that several subjects did not understand the difference between questions 1 and 3, so that the data were considered too unreliable for use.

One further point should perhaps be noted with reference to budget group A in that it required some special handling and treatment. In order to differentiate between Groups Aβ and Aγ, the Aγ subjects were asked first to guess what the budget would be and then, assuming this to be the actual goal, form their aspirations. The presence of a goal

---

[1]Analyses of supplementary (motivational) questionnaires indicates that the procedure employed had some undesirable effects in that some of the subjects felt a sense of futility in forming and stating aspirations which they perceived as having no normative consequences. The results indicate, however, that these subjects underestimated the effects of the mere formation of these aspiration levels on their performance.

[2]This may have given this group some advantage, not merely because of the (slight) saving in time and energy, but also because of the fact that it was not required to divert attention to matters other than the immediate task. On the other hand (even though the literature of budgeting is largely silent on this point), this kind of advantage may be associated with a lack of need for stating aspiration levels as well as other "attention diverting" procedures that are associated with normal budgetary practice. (In this connection see also the preceding footnote.)

[3]Through the use of question 3 on questionnaires given to β and γ subjects. See Exhibits 4A.3 — 4A.7, pp. 103–104.

was thus made more evident in the Aγ than the Aβ group during the aspiration level formation. Group Aγ subjects received a piece of paper before each test which was merely a reminder of the existence of the budget.

4.5. Experimental Procedure

The subjects were tested in groups, ranging in size from four to seventeen. Since the aspiration level groupings required different types of paper distribution and instructions during the interim periods, it was necessary to run each group of subjects as all α, all β, or all γ. However, all budget groups were represented in each group, the alphabetical ordering of the groups following some convenient path around the experimental room. Care was taken, however, to avoid bias in placing the subjects — e.g., the kind of bias that might be associated with placing all of the Group A members in the front row.

The seating of the subjects, reading and explanation of the instructions, the first aspiration level determination (in Group β and γ), and the first budget distribution consumed about twenty minutes. After each test (of seven minute duration) there was an interim scoring period which varied between seven and twelve minutes[1] during which a discussion was conducted either on some topic the group was studying or the campus redevelopment program. This was designed to provide rest for the subjects as well as to avoid discussion of the experiment — as the amount of information dispensed would have been impossible to control from group to group. After the sixth test, a questionnaire designed to evaluate some general reactions of the subjects to the experiment was distributed.[2] The total running time for the experiment averaged two hours, varying about fifteen minutes in either direction.

4.6. Structure of the Design and Subjects Utilized

The number of factors to be considered and the number of replications desired required careful consideration, at least from a statistical and resource requirement standpoint, since otherwise a forbiddingly

---

[1]Depending upon the size of the group and the experience of the scorers. During the five days in which the experiments were run the efficiency of test scoring increased considerably. However, the aspiration level groupings were well scattered throughout the period so that no consistent bias was likely to have been introduced as a result.

[2]A specimen is included in Appendix 4A, q.v.

complex and time consuming task would be confronted. In brief, the design involved 12 groupings (3 aspiration levels and 4 budget types) performed over 9 replicates giving 108 subjects, each involving 6 trials (or tests), for a total of 648 observations to be analyzed. Thus, in statistical jargon, the design used was a "6 × 3 × 4 factorial design with 9 replicates." In this context issues of convenience were sometimes favored over statistical niceties such as efficient designs and test power (relative to Type II error).[1]

All 108 subjects were students at the Carnegie Institute of Technology and all but 9 were studying management or administration. The range of subjects covered by year of college level attained ran the gamut from sophomore undergraduates to second-year graduate students.[2] In order to prevent large-scale information dissemination which might affect the performance of later relative to earlier subjects), two procedures were followed which necessitated running the subjects in large, homogeneous groups: (1) the tests were run over the shortest feasible (five-day) period, and (2) subjects who were most likely to have contact with one another were run simultaneously. This resulted in some confounding of the aspiration level groupings with subject classifications. However, this was in part controlled by having each set of replicates balanced (e.g., sophomore undergraduates offset by second year graduates) so that the effect of such heterogeneity would, in general, be reflected in an inflation of the remainder sum of squares and thereby compensate for a possible increase in the sum of squares due to the confounding of the aspiration level groups.[3]

---

[1]Actually, the question of Type II error in purely scientific work is not a wholly settled one in statistics. (See, for instance, R. A. Fisher's review (32) of A. Wald.) But, of course, such questions would, in general, be highly relevant for applied work and would naturally lead towards something like the sequential designs developed by H. Robbins and others (65) as an outgrowth of the principles underlying modern statistical decision theory as developed by A. Wald (83) and others.

[2]Of the students studying management, 12 were senior electrical engineering students in a management option curriculum, 42 were undergraduate students in Industrial Management, and 45 were graduate students in Industrial Administration. The remaining 9 consisted of 4 seniors in electrical engineering or physics and 5 advanced graduate students in electrical or chemical engineering.

[3]The classification of subjects in experimental groups is shown in Appendix 4A. An a priori measure of the group ability was assumed to be "aggregate years of study" — i.e., sophomore undergraduate = 2, junior = 3, etc., up to second year or more advanced graduate = 6. This quantity was limited to a range of 36 to 41 except for Group Aα which was low (32) and although not the lowest in performance, was low compared with what might have been expected.

4.7. Analysis of Results — Performances

The criterion of effectiveness of a particular combination of aspiration level determination and budget level was considered, in the light of the reasoning of Section 4.2, to be the average number of problems solved by the group per trial. A tabulation of this variate, by groups, is given in Table 4.1.[1] The significance of the group differences in performance was tested, as usual, under what, in statistical jargon, is called the "linear hypothesis:"[2]

$$(4.7.1) \qquad y_{ijkl} = \mu + t_i + a_j + b_k + (ta)_{ij} + (tb)_{ik} \\ + (ab)_{jk} + (tab)_{ijk} + e_{ijkl}$$

$$i = 1, ..., 6; \; j = 1, ..., 3; \; k = 1, ..., 4; \; l = 1, ..., 9$$

where

y_{ijkl} = performance of the lth individual on the ith test in the jth aspiration level group and the kth budget group

$(4.7.2) \quad \mu$ = universe mean (average performance)

t_i = effect of the ith test on performance

a_j = effect of the jth aspiration level group on performance

b_k = effect of the kth budget group on performance

TABLE 4.1. AVERAGE NUMBER OF PROBLEMS SOLVED PER TEST BY EXPERIMENTAL GROUPS CLASSIFIED ACCORDING TO BUDGET TYPE AND ASPIRATION LEVEL DETERMINATION.

Aspiration Level / Budget	α Budget Only	β Aspiration, then Budget	γ Budget, then Aspiration	Average all Aspirations
A — Implicit	4.56	5.41	5.60	5.18
B — Low	4.09	4.70	4.56	4.45
C — Medium	4.35	5.45	5.50	5.10
D — High	5.13	4.04	5.85	5.01
Average all Budgets	4.53	4.90	5.39	4.94

Note: Each of the subgroup averages represents the performance of 9 subjects in 6 tests = 54 observations.

---

[1] A more complete tabulation, showing total group scores on each test is given in Appendix 4B.

[2] This should not be confused with the assumption (not made) that the relations to be tested are linear. See H. B. Mann (55), pp. 23, 24.

and where $(ta)_{ij}$ is the effect on performance of the interaction of the ith test and the jth aspiration level grouping which cannot be attributed to the sum of the separate (main) effects, etc. The term e_{ijkl} is a random error term, and in accord with standard statistical assumptions the errors are assumed to have zero expected value, and to be uncorrelated and homoscedastic. All other terms, save μ, have zero first moments, and $E(a_i^2) = \sigma_a^2$, so that they, too, are homoscedastic.[1]

In general, it is assumed that the (mathematical and statistical) parts of the general Markoff theorem are satisfied[2] and an analysis of variance, using the F-test may be employed. The results are as summarized in Table 4.2. The data indicate that a subject's performance is significantly affected by his budget, the way in which he determines his aspiration

TABLE 4.2.   ANALYSIS OF VARIANCE — PERFORMANCE

Due to	Sum of Squares	Degrees of Freedom	Mean Square	Variance Ratio (F)
Main Effects: Tests (t)	1557.500	5	311.500	59.706†
Aspiration Levels (a)	77.121	2	38.561	7.391†
Budgets (b)	53.315	3	17.772	3.406*
Interactions (2-way): Tests × Aspirations (ta)	22.324	10	2.232	.428
Tests × Budgets (tb)	21.728	15	1.449	.278
Aspirations × Budgets (ab)	100.323	6	16.721	3.205†
Interactions (3-way): Tests × Aspirations × Budgets (tab)	63.856	30	2.129	.408
Error (Remainder)	3005.111	576	5.217	. . .
Total	4901.278	647	. . .	. . .

†Denotes highly significant (1 per cent level)
*Denotes significant (5 per cent level)

---

[1]See, for example, Kempthorn (41), Chapter 6; or Davies (25), Chapter 8.
[2]See Kempthorn, *op. cit.*, Chapter V ff.

level (e.g., before or after receiving budgetary information), and the combination of the two. There was a highly significant test effect but the magnitude of the differences between tests did not appear to be affected by the groupings — as indicated by the nonsignificance of the (*ta*) and (*tb*) interactions.

Thus, it is possible to attach significance to the ordering of the performance by budget and aspiration level group. For notation purposes, let "$X > Y$" indicate that the subjects of Group X performed better (on the average) than the subjects of Group Y. Then, referring to Table 4.1, the relations

(4.7.3a) $A > C > D > B$

and

(4.7.3b) $\gamma > \beta > \alpha$

are obtained. Thus the implicit budget group performed best, the medium budget group next, then the high budget group, and finally the low budget group.

The group that determined its aspirations with knowledge of the budgeted goal (which was, on the average, higher than performance on all but the sixth test) performed better than the group without this knowledge and still better than the group which did not explicitly formulate its aspirations.

Although the differences between the aspiration level groups taken in pairs are significant at the 2 per cent level or better and the differences between the low budget (B) and the other budget groups are significant at the .2 per cent level or better, the differences between A, C, and D taken in pairs are not particularly reliable.[1] Thus the ordering, $A > C > D$, can be inferred from the sample as the most probable ordering, but it is impossible to reject the null hypothesis, i.e., $A = C = D$.

Referring again to Table 4.1, the extremes of the table are $D\gamma$ and $D\beta$. This difference is estimated to be in the neighborhood of 6 standard deviations of the distribution of the sample mean and accounts in large measure for the superiority of γ performance over β performance.

An hypothesis which would serve to explain this difference is as

---

[1]Assuming the sample means to be normally distributed and using the mean square error as the estimate of the population variance. The number of degrees of freedom for budgets (322) and aspiration levels (430) is sufficiently large to justify the assumption of normality. The probability of significant difference is shown in more detail in Appendix 4B, p. 108.

follows: the Dγ group formed its aspirations with the knowledge of the "high" management budget and hence tended somewhat to accept it as its own; the Dβ group formed its aspirations prior to receiving its budgets in the light of previous performance, and when the high budget arrived mentally (i.e., psychologically) rejected it.

Internal support for this hypothesis is available from analyzing the data on the relationship of the budget to performance. Although the budgets for the Dβ group were considerably lower than those for the Dγ group (since they depended upon prior performance), the Dβ subjects as a group attained the budget only 9 times during the entire test (or an average of 1 attainment per subject), while the Dγ subjects attained the budget 19 times (or an average of 2.1 attainments per subject).

An extension of this hypothesis to explain the superiority of Bβ over Bγ is, however, more dubious. The hypothesis would imply that the Bβ subjects, having previously stated their aspiration levels, would reject the budget as being too low and would strive for higher scores. The Bβ subjects as a group attained the budget more often (3.7 attainments per subject) than the Bγ subjects (3.2 attainments per subject), which would imply, if anything, that the Bβ subjects were influenced by the budget to a greater extent. On the other hand, the Bβ group performances exceeded both their budgets and their aspiration levels by far more than did those of the Bγ group, so that the situation is not at all clear. The budget attainments of Cβ and Cγ are almost identical (3.1 and 3.2 attainments per subject respectively), as were their performances, so that little can be gained from further comparisons of this type.[1]

A note is in order regarding the overall performance of the subjects. Performance, p, can be expressed as a linear function of the number of the test, t, as follows:

$$(4.7.4) \qquad p_t = 2.37 + \underset{(\pm.0571)}{.732}\, t \text{ where } t = 1, \ldots, 6.$$

However, a component analysis of variance, as set forth in Appendix 4B, indicates that the quadratic and cubic components are also significant, so that the relation:

$$(4.7.5) \quad p_t = -0.65 + 5.71\, t - 1.98\, t^2 + .212\, t^3$$
$$\text{or}$$
$$\left. \begin{aligned} p_t = 4.22 &- .338\, (t - \bar{t}) + .248\, (t - \bar{t})^2 \\ &+ .212\, (t - \bar{t})^3 \end{aligned} \right\} t = 1, \ldots, 6;\ \bar{t} = 3.5$$

___

[1]It should also be reported, for the sake of completeness, that Aβ subjects averaged 2.6 attainments per subject, group Aγ 2 attainments per subject. For groups Aα, Bα, Cα, and Dα, the figures are 2.1, 2.8, 2.7, and 2.6 attainments per subject, respectively.

would appear to describe the performance curve fairly well. Any extrapolation of this curve would be unwarranted, however, since the maximum performance of 15 problems would be exceeded on a (hypo-

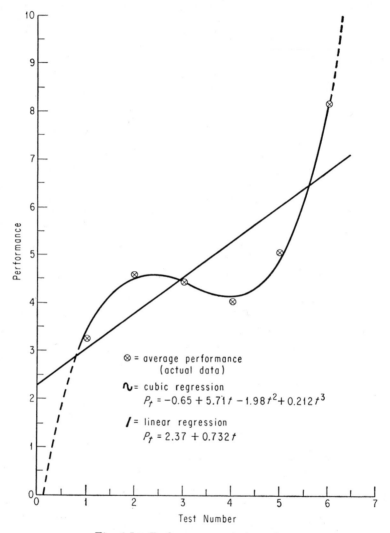

Fig. 4.1.   Performance vs test number.

thetical) seventh test. However, comparing the cubic with the linear trend in Figure 4.1, it would appear that some guesses might be ventured about the difficulty of the tests.

In particular, it might be guessed that test 4 was probably the most difficult test,[1] Tests 2 or 6 the easiest. So much for inferences from simple appearances of the curve plotted through the observations relative to the straight line shown. Furthermore, if an exponential learning curve had been considered, Test 5 might well be above the reference curve (the exponential) so that the apparent case might be deceptive.

In order to determine the possible effects of the difficulty of the test on the relative performance of the groups, a variance analysis was performed on the individual tests,[2] but the results can only be suggestive. The highly significant differences in performance appear to be a result of the performance on Tests 3 and 5 (in which aspiration level groupings are significant) and Test 6 (on which the probability of a difference is at least finite). Finite probabilities of a difference between budget groups exist in Tests 2 and 6, and (*ab*) interactions appear possible on Tests 3 and 6.

On Tests 1 and 4 the grouping of the data serves only to increase the variance estimate,[3] which would suggest that the difference between the groups initially was insignificant, and the difficult task, 6, rather than accentuating the differences appears to have reduced them.

4.8. Analysis of Results — Aspiration Level

In order to investigate in more detail the possible causes of the differences in performance noted between groups, the data which were acquired on the aspiration levels of the subjects may next be examined. The measure of aspiration level which will be used is the subject's answer to the question, "How many problems do you hope to complete on Test X?"[4]

The aspiration level on Test 1 was formulated by the subjects with incomplete information about the tasks. Group β had only the two

---

[1]The "difficulty" of Test 4 was undoubtedly enhanced by other factors: (1) subjects who had been unsuccessful on three consecutive trials had no money at all; (2) the sequence of budget adjustments produced the higher of the two "adjustments" so that the discrepancy between the budget and the perceived possible achievement may have been sufficiently large to cause many subjects to "give up;" and (3) a few subjects who had formed some estimate of the budget-setting procedure and the discrepancy noted in (2) may have been induced by them to use Test 4 to "try it out."

[2]As indicated in Appendix 4B.

[3]In fact, a result $F < 1$ is obtained.

[4]It will be recalled that this question was asked only of group β and γ subjects, thus reducing the sample for this discussion to 72.

sample problems on which to base their aspirations; Group Aγ had little more,[1] but the Bγ, Cγ, and Dγ groups received their budget of 5 problems prior to formulating their aspiration levels.[2] Either because the sample problems were easier than the test problems or because they were perceived as being easier[3] — or perhaps because of some other factor —, the group β subjects' average aspiration level was 8.5 problems, compared with a performance average of 3. Group Aγ subjects' average aspiration level was 6.6 compared with a performance of 3.2, but the subjects who had received the budget of 5 had an average aspiration of 5.9 compared with a performance of 3.5.[4]

Perhaps even more indicative of the attraction power of the budget in the incomplete information situation is the comparison of the number of people who chose the number "5" for their aspiration level on the first test. Only 1 of 36 Group β subjects chose 5, although five chose numbers below 5; in group Aγ, 2 subjects chose 5 (and 3 subjects a number below 5); in the combined Bγ, Cγ, and Dγ groups, 11 subjects out of 27 chose 5 but only 1 subject chose a number below 5. It is also interesting to note that 6 people in the β group chose 15 (maximum possible), and no subject in Bγ, Cγ, or Dγ did so.

Thus the budget, in the absence of complete information about the task, became the aspiration level for more than one-third of the subjects.

---

[1] It is possible that a few of the Aγ subjects may have spied the budgets of 5 received by the other γ subjects in the same room. In the absence of information, the subjects' curiosity in some cases was difficult to control.

[2] Thus all of the Group β subjects may be considered as a single homogeneous group for the first aspiration level determination; Bγ, Cγ, and Dγ are likewise a homogeneous grouping; but Aγ constitutes a third group.

[3] Once the solution to a water-jar problem is "seen" the problem usually seems trivial. Since the sample problems were already solved on the instruction sheet, the real task — i.e., discovering the solution — had already been performed and the subjects may have included only the time they thought necessary to write down the solution in their estimates. Although the sample problems may have been easier than some of the problems at the end of the test, only a few of the subjects solved enough problems on the first test even to attempt the problems which may have been more difficult than the sample.

[4] The difference between the mean aspiration level of the β subjects and the γ subjects (excluding Aγ) was significant at the 1 per cent level. The β group was much more variable than the combined Bγ, Cγ, and Dγ groups in its aspiration, and the ratio (β/γ) of the sums of squares (adjusted by the appropriate degrees of freedom) is significantly greater than 1 at the .1 per cent level. The estimates of the population variance from the two samples were $\hat{\sigma}^2 = 15.1$ and $\hat{\sigma}^2 = 1.62$ for β and γ (excluding Aγ) respectively.

This same information would appear to have eliminated subjects who might have otherwise aspired to the maximum (technological optimum) score. Finally, it (1) significantly *lowered* the average aspiration level and (2) caused a significant decrease of variability of the aspiration level about its average value.[1] A question remains, of course, as to whether a budget which was higher than the average of the β group aspirations — say, a budget of 10 or 12 correctly completed problems — would have significantly raised the aspiration level of the γ groups.[2]

Two factors are of interest in comparing the performance of the two groups. In spite of the high level of aspiration, the β groups performed, on the average, .52 problems less than the Bγ, Cγ, and Dγ combination. (It should be observed, however, that the null hypothesis cannot be rejected in this case at even the 10 per cent significance level.) The β groups, however, in the absence of an externally imposed factor, appeared in some degree to reflect their abilities, at least relative to one another, in their aspiration level determination, while the groups which were influenced by the budget did not.

This last phenomenon is exhibited by the correlation estimates. The coefficient of correlation between aspiration level and performance for

---

[1]Actually, it was possible to reject the null hypothesis ($\mu = 5$) in either group even at the 1 per cent level. For the sake of exposition, 5 per cent confidence limits for the two groups were:

$$7.22 \leq \mu \leq 9.86 \qquad \text{for the } \beta \text{ group}$$

$$5.42 \leq \mu \leq 6.44 \qquad \text{for B}\gamma, \text{C}\gamma, \text{ and D}\gamma \text{ groups combined}$$

Thus it is apparent that the budget presented in the absence of other information *influenced*, but did not necessarily *become*, the aspiration level. The obvious difficulties which accrue from aggregation here require further study beyond the scope of this thesis.

[2]It is of interest here to compare these results with those of Chapman and Volkmann (7). Their experiment involving aspiration levels in the absence of information about the task (summarized on pp. 44-45 of this thesis) showed a reluctance on the part of the subjects to aspire even to the average performance of "unselected WPA workers." On the other hand, the subjects of the experiment presented here aspired to a level on the average higher than the stated goal which corresponds to the Chapman and Volkmann group norm insofar as it is the only figure which the subjects can use as a reference point. Although this difference between the subjects of the two experiments can be explained entirely in terms of differences in subjects and experimental procedures, the possibility exists that in spite of attempts by the experimenter, subjects will develop some intuitive (if irrational) performance estimates prior to their first encounter with the task. These a priori estimates appear to be fairly easily changed by experience with the task but resist change from an external source, at least to some extent.

the β subjects was .436 (significant at the 1 per cent level),[1] while for $B\gamma$, $C\gamma$, and $D\gamma$ subjects, the correlation was negative ($-.063$) but not significantly different from 0. Group $A\gamma$ had an average performance of 3.2. This was closer to β than to the other γ groups and also resembled the β group in its aspiration performance correlation of .318 (significant at the 5 per cent level) and its variance ($\hat{\sigma}^2 = 15.3$).

It may be then hypothesized that, in the absence of complete information about the task, some ranking of aspiration levels relative to maximum and minimum values occurs and that this ranking reflects the abilities of the individuals — at least relative to one another — and, finally, that the imposition of an external goal interferes with this ranking. The alternate hypothesis, viz., that the aspiration level which is set without reference to an external goal has a greater effect on performance than one which is seen, at least partially, to be forced upon the individual,[2] does not receive much support since γ performance was superior to β performance. On the other hand, the inferiority of β performance may support the existence of a point of maximum stress hypothesized above (Postulate (iii.a) of Chapter 2), but it must be admitted that the evidence is not conclusive. Furthermore, in viewing these results the problem of bias due to the disparity of educational level of the subjects noted above must be considered.

It should be observed that possible interference with aspiration level determination, due to learning about the next test before it is administered, may occur, in that the subjects appeared to become more adept at solving the problems as the test trials progressed (at least for the number of tests used). On the other hand, it is unlikely that the incremental gain in information about the task, which would aid in determination of the aspiration level, is significant on any test other than the first.[3] Hence it is possible to group the aspiration levels from Tests 2 to 6 together as "informed" levels.

There appeared to be relatively little difficulty in dislodging the

---

[1]This result is consistent with the results of Chapman and Volkmann (7) (discussed in Chapter 3 of this thesis). They, too, found that in their control group (which had no external information other than minimum and maximum possible scores) the subjects' performance and aspirations were positively and significantly correlated.

[2]This seems to be the import — as nearly as can be ascertained — of the suggestions and comments made by Argyris (2).

[3]I.e., it is unlikely that the subject possesses any more information at the end of Test 3 about Test 4 (relative to his ability) than he had at the end of Test 2 about Test 3 (although he probably has more information about Test 4, relative to his ability than he had at the end of Test 2).

subjects from the initial aspiration level once the first test had been performed. Of the 72 subjects whose aspirations were requested, only 9 duplicated their original choices on the second test. Of the 9, two were γ subjects whose choice was reinforced by having their budgets coincide with the previous aspiration level. Three others maintained the same aspiration level throughout.[1]

The small number of duplications and the attached mitigating statements tend to indicate that (since the expected value of the number of repetitions, assuming the choices independent, is $\frac{1}{15} \times 72 = 4.8$) the first aspiration level choice does not substantially affect subsequent choices, except in cases of extreme "rigidity" for which the circumstances of the first choice are vital. Since the cases in which no change at all occurred in the aspiration level numbered only 3, or 4 per cent of the sample, it is not likely that the results of the study of the "informed" aspiration level would have been drastically changed if the aspiration level determination for the first test would have been eliminated.

Uncovering or discovering causal factors in a statistical analysis drawn from such a model design is a somewhat tricky business. For this purpose, the following suggested procedure might be employed in this case. To distinguish causal relationships that may exist with regard to the formulation of the aspiration level and its subsequent effect on performance, two types of discrepancies might be distinguished for analysis. Lewin et al. (37b) have defined the difference between the aspiration level for a test and the score on the test as the "achievement discrepancy," while the difference between the aspiration level and the performance on the previous test is called the "goal discrepancy." In a

---

[1]This phenomenon has been investigated thoroughly by Rotter (67) and others using the "Level of Aspiration Board" which involves a task of rolling a steel ball along a groove. Terming this absence of shifts the "rigid pattern," Rotter states: "Rigidity here is to be thought of as primarily an avoidance response — a way of avoiding decisions or situations in which commitment may lead to a mistake or punishment." ((67), p. 322.) Six other subjects shifted after the first test but retained the level chosen for the second test thereafter; these would also fit Rotter's definition of the "rigid pattern." It is interesting to note that all cases of rigidity occurred in the β groups and Group Aγ. Assuming an average occurrence of rigidity to be $\frac{9}{72} = \frac{1}{8}$ for the entire group, the probability that all 9 would occur in 5 groups (45 subjects), or that 3 groups (27 subjects) would contain no cases of rigidity is C_{27}^{63}/C_{27}^{72} or about .010. This assumes a finite population. If, alternately, an infinite population were assumed with rigidity occurring in $\frac{1}{8}$ of the population, then the estimate of the chance probability of drawing 27 without rigidity would be $(\frac{7}{8})^{27} \cong$ .027. Hence it must be concluded from these data and for this experiment that an externally imposed goal prior to the formation of aspirations significantly reduces "rigidity."

situation in which the amount of performance improvement per trial is small, the difference between the two discrepancies will be small and is usually ignored.[1] If a continuous model is assumed (e.g., the model of Chapter 2) the discrepancies must be identical.

The model of causality assumed for present purposes is shown in Figure 4.2. It will be noted that, as in the mathematical model, the

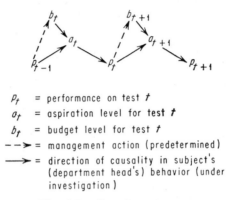

p_t = performance on test t
a_t = aspiration level for test t
b_t = budget level for test t
--→ = management action (predetermined)
——→ = direction of causality in subject's (department head's) behavior (under investigation)

Fig. 4.2. Causality relations.

budget is assumed to work through the aspiration level to performance rather than directly.

Studies of the goal discrepancy in the absence of a budget have shown that its magnitude can be reliably predicted from an independent study of personality.[2] In the absence of a priori indications of differences in personality between groups[3] it may be concluded that if the between group differences in goal discrepancy are significant, it will be possible to establish a causal relationship leading from the type of budget and/or aspiration level determination to the goal discrepancy. Since the previous performance is an exogenous variable at the time of aspiration level determination, the causal relationship can be extended to the aspiration level.

---

[1]See, for example, Rotter (67), Chapter II, particularly pp. 128-130, and Chapter VIII, pp. 313-326.

[2]*Ibid.*

[3]Actually, the extremes of the subject classifications were largely confined to the α groups, and noting Table 4A, the β and γ subgroups differed for the most part in terms of whether the 3 or 4 seniors in the group were studying management in the regular curriculum or on an elective basis.

The goal discrepancy analysis of variance[1] shows that the differences between budget groups are highly significant as are the three-way interactions. The latter can be accounted for by the budget setting procedure. The goal discrepancy followed a strong regular pattern in the Bγ, Cγ, and Dγ groups which was absent in the others.[2] The fact that the test effect was not significant would tend to validate the assumption made above, viz. that the amount of additional information received about the task on tests other than the first is small.

Returning to Table 4.3, it is seen that the average goal discrepancy *exceeded* the "ideal" goal discrepancy (which would occur if management could control the aspirations exactly as $a_t = b_t$) in the A groups and Bγ but was below the "ideal" elsewhere. The amount of the difference between "ideal" and actual discrepancy increased with the severity of the budget in the Bγ, Cβ, and Dγ groups, but decreased in the Bγ, Cβ, and Dβ groups. Taken together, these statements would imply that the more explicit information at the time of formulation of the aspiration level tended to mitigate rather than accentuate the differences between budgets. Unfortunately, however, significant (ab) interactions, which would be required for validity of this conclusion, are not present.

The achievement discrepancy analysis of variance[3] showed highly significant test and budget effects. Since the test effect of the goal discrepancy is not significant, the ranking of the achievement discrepancy can be assumed to be a reasonably accurate measure of the differences in difficulty between tests. The ranking indicates the order of difficulty as 4, 3, 2, 5, 6, which is in accord with the comments in Section 4.7. This achievement discrepancy is comparable with the discrepancy which is considered to be a measure of stress in Chapter 2 (i.e., frustration is evoked in the attempt to perform at a level of aspiration (already set) above ability, not in the process of setting the aspiration[4]).

Comparing Tables 4.3 and 4.1, it may be noted that the average test scores from 2 — 6 preserve the same ranking by subgroups as the scores

---

[1]Table 4B.8 of the Appendix.

[2]As will be recalled, the budgets were set by adding a number (1 or 0 for Group B, 2 or 1 for Group C, etc.) to the previous score. The higher of the two numbers always occurred on tests 2, 4, and 6. Subjects in Groups Bγ, Cγ, and Dγ (having seen the budget) often set their aspirations at, or a fixed number below or above, the budget. Thus the goal discrepancies of these subjects followed the high-low pattern of the alternating budgets, while this effect did not (and would not be expected to) prevail in other groups.

[3]Table 4B.9 of the Appendix.

[4]Ruch (68), Chapter 7.

TABLE 4.3. AVERAGE PERFORMANCE, GOAL DISCREPANCY, AND ACHIEVEMENT DISCREPANCY

Average of:	Aspir. Group	Budget Group				A + B + C + D
		A	B	C	D	
Performance, Tests 1 — 5	β	4.70	4.07	4.74	3.63	4.28
+ Goal Discrepancy		+1.94	+0.09	+1.22	+2.35	+1.40
= Aspiration Level		6.64	4.16	5.96	5.98	5.68
− Achievement Discrepancy		−0.82	+0.94	−0.09	−1.67	−0.41
= Performance, Tests 2 — 6		5.82	5.10	5.87	4.31	5.27
Performance, Tests 1 — 5	γ	4.81	3.95	4.85	5.18	4.70
+ Goal Discrepancy		+1.38	+0.76	+1.11	+1.49	+1.19
= Aspiration Level		6.19	4.71	5.96	6.67	5.89
− Achievement Discrepancy		−0.13	+0.16	−0.09	−0.45	−0.13
= Performance, Tests 2 — 6		6.06	4.87	5.87	6.22	5.76
Performance, Tests 1 — 5	β + γ	4.76	4.01	4.80	4.41	4.49
+ Goal Discrepancy		+1.66	+0.43	+1.16	+1.91	+1.29
= Aspiration Level		6.42	4.44	5.96	6.32	5.78
− Achievement Discrepancy		−0.48	+0.55	−0.09	−1.06	−0.27
= Performance, Tests 2 — 6		5.94	4.99	5.87	5.26	5.51
"Ideal" Goal Discrepancy $a_t = b_t$		1.60	0.60	1.60	2.60	1.60

for 1 — 6 except that the insignificant difference between Cγ and Cβ is eliminated. It should be noted that stress in D exceeded stress in C and A, although performance was ranked A > C > D > B. The ranking of budget groups and Dγ, viz. Dγ > A > C > B, also does not quite correspond with the stress (achievement discrepancy) ranking for those groups, in that stress in Dγ is less than stress in A. However, the relationship between stress and performance may have some validity since the functional dependence of performance and achievement discrepancy produces an influence counter to the ordering shown, and a somewhat altered measure of stress might produce more reliable results. The Dβ group, and/or some of the subjects in it, may exhibit the phenomenon of stress exceeding some maximum limit. (See postulates (iii) of the model in Chapter 2). Although not conclusive, the results suggest that the effect of higher stress, up to a point, is to increase performance.

The study of the achievement discrepancy is somewhat disappointing insofar as no definite conclusions can be drawn other than an estimate of the difficulty of the tests. On the other hand, if the achievement discrepancy is a measure of stress, then a task which is considerably more difficult than usual may cause stress to exceed some tolerable value.[1] Furthermore, this difficult task may appear (as it did here) without either the intention or the knowledge of management.

4.9. Conclusions

The results of the experiment have shown that performance in a situation where the attainment of a goal is rewarded and its nonattainment penalized is significantly affected by the type of budget chosen, the conditions of administration, and the way in which aspiration levels for the task are determined.

The experimental results indicate that an "implicit" budget (where the subject is not told what goal he must attain) produces the best performance, closely followed by a "medium" budget and a "high" budget. The "low" budget, which was the only one which satisfied the criterion of "attainable but not too loose," resulted in performance significantly lower than the other budget groups.

However, there is a strong interaction effect between budgets and the aspiration level determination grouping. The group of "high" budget subjects who received their budgets prior to setting their aspiration levels perfomed better than any other group, whereas the "high" budget group

---

[1]See remarks in Sections 2.3 and 2.4 regarding stress.

who set their aspirations before receiving the budget were the lowest performers of any group.

An hypothesis which might satisfactorily explain this phenomenon is as follows: The high performing group formed its aspirations with the high budget levels in mind, while the low performing group rejected the high budget after forming aspirations with relation to their last performance. However, aspiration level data indicate that the low performing group had a much higher goal discrepancy so that, if anything, their goals were closer, on the average, to the budget than were the high performers.

The low performing group also had a very high achievement discrepancy score. If achievement discrepancy is interpreted as a measure of stress, this would give rise to an alternate hypothesis — viz. that the stress, at least for some subjects, was so high that they may have been "discouraged" and may have ceased to try to improve performance.

A major difficulty is involved in the use of achievement discrepancy scores. This results from the functional dependency of such scores upon performance. For example, a constant aspiration level would produce a negative correlation between achievement discrepancy and performance (ignoring the trivial case where performance equals aspiration level throughout). This conceptual deficiency of the current state of psychological theorizing makes it difficult to establish a causal relationship between this discrepancy and performance — as hypothesized in this model. It is, however, significant that the ordering of the stress (achievement discrepancy) corresponded fairly closely to the ordering of performance in spite of the opposing effect of the functional dependency.

It is also observed from the analysis that the size of the achievement discrepancy can be affected significantly by the size of the budget, a result which is consistent with the requirements for the validity of postulate (ii) in the model of Chapter 2.

The investigation of the goal discrepancy also indicated a significant budget effect, and this again tends to corroborate postulate (ii), since in the continuous model the two discrepancies are indistinguishable. A somewhat surprising (even though not statistically significant) effect is also present. This is the tendency of the groups who formed their aspiration levels without knowledge of the budget to come closer to their budget than is true for the group which had the advantage of the budget information supplied to them. A possible explanation is that a moderate departure from the budget can come about gradually in the groups that form aspirations first, while a departure in the other groups (since the budget is associated with reward) is likely to be a large shift downward.

The types of aspiration levels, under the procedures used, did play a part in performance differences. This was to be expected. But the fact that it did not play a part in the discrepancies which occurred requires some explanation. One possibility is that the greater variability of the aspirations noted in the aspirations of the β subjects (who did not have the budget when forming their aspirations), in spite of roughly the same average aspirations, may have produced a greater number of discouraged subjects (who had aspired to extremely high levels). In the group whose aspiration levels tended to remain close to the budget, there were relatively few extremely high or low discrepancies. Hence this group would tend to exhibit high but not intolerable levels which, according to postulates stated earlier, would lead to high performance as well.

Although not conclusive on the point, the study does shed some light on participative schemes of budgetary management insofar as these are connected to aspiration levels. The group which determines its aspiration level first, in the experimental situation, is closest to the solution proposed by MacGregor (54). He suggests that the department head should plan his budget and then take it to his supervisor who will give him his budget based on his estimate. The experimental data raise some questions as to the universal validity of this recommendation, for under the experimental situation if "management" decides on a "high" (performance) budget, its use of MacGregor's participation plan coincides with the worst possible result. On the other hand, it would probably help performance in a "low" budget situation.

This summary of the findings may now be concluded by a few observations on the causal connection between stress and performance. As already noted, the experiment did help to separate and distinguish between goal discrepancy and achievement discrepancy. The best that the data and subsequent analyses will bear on the subject of "stress" suggests only the possible use of achievement discrepancy as either a surrogate or a direct measure of stress. The value of the achievement discrepancy as a measure of stress is dubious and the effect of stress and/or achievement discrepancy on performance requires further documentation before such usage is fully warranted.

DETAILS OF THE EXPERIMENTAL DESIGN

4A.1. Task Selection

The capacities for the three jars were chosen from a table of random numbers, 1 to 50 inclusive, eliminating duplications (in the same problem) when they occurred. A "solution" was then selected at random from a prepared set of nine possible solutions. Some selection of a parent population was necessarily and unavoidably involved at this stage. The criterion employed was an initial judgment that each set to be sampled was fairly close in order of difficulty. As a precaution, preliminary or pilot tests were conducted, but these could not be undertaken on a sufficient scale to empirically compare the results of the selection process with the criterion of equal difficulty of the tests. In any event the population (of solutions) so chosen was used for the random draws and a requirement determined accordingly.

In more detail this phase of the design was as follows: the solution for problem 1 was chosen at random from groups 1, 2, and 3 of Table 4A.1. In like manner the solution for problem 2 was chosen from groups 2, 3, and 4, etc. In this table the letters A, B, and C refer to the largest, middle, and smallest jars, respectively. (In the actual test A, B, and C are listed as they occurred in the table of random numbers.) If the solution chosen produced an impossible requirement for a set of capacities (e.g., the requirement 2A cannot be obtained if $A > B + C$), another solution was chosen at random from the remaining eight, and so on until the desired test battery was complete.[1]

---

[1] In every case at least one of the solutions possessed a feasible requirement, although there was no guarantee of this.

TABLE 4A.1. REQUIRED AMOUNTS IN TERMS OF JAR CAPACITIES $(A > B > C)$ — LISTED IN APPROXIMATE ORDER OF DIFFICULTY.*

Group 1	$A + B + C$, $2B$, $2C$	3
Group 2	$A - B$, $A - C$, $B - C$	3
Group 3	$2B + C$, $A + 2C$, $B + 2C$	4
Group 4	$A - B + C$, $A + B - C$, $2A$	4
Group 5	$A - 2C$, $3C$, $3B(A < 2B)$	5
Group 6	$A - 2B$, $2B - A$, $B - 2C$	5
Group 7	$2C - B$, $2B - C$, $2C - A$	5
Group 8	$B + C - A$, $2A - B(A < 2B)$, $A - B - C$	5
Group 9	$2A - C$, $2A - B(A > 2B)$, $3B(A < 2B)$	6
Group 10	$A + 3C$, $B + 3C$, $3B + C$	6
Group 11	$2B + 2C$, $A + B - 2C$, $A - B + 2C$	6
Group 12	$B + 2C - A(A < B + C)$, $2B + C - A(A < 2B)$,	
	$A - 2B + C(A < 2B)$	6
Group 13	$4C(A > 2C)$ $4B(A < 4B)$ $A - 3C$	7
Group 14	$A - 3B$, $B - 3C$, $3C - B$	7
Group 15	$3B - A$, $2B - 2C$, $2A - 2C$	7
Group 16	$2A - 2B(A < 3B + C)$, $A - 2B - C$, $A - B - 2C$	7
Group 17	$B + 2C - A(A > B + C)$, $2B + C - A(A < 2B)$,	
	$A - 2B + C(A < 2B)$	7
Group 18†	$2A - B - C$, $2A - 2B(A < 3B)$, $3B - C(2B - C < A)$	7

*Items in parentheses denote restrictions on the jar capacities which allow the problem to be solved in the indicated number of steps — restrictions for the existence of a solution are omitted.

†Shown for completeness; all other problems require 8 or more steps.

The selection process was intended to give a rough ordering (in terms of increasing difficulty) from the first to the last problem on any test. Actually, it is almost impossible to determine a priori a precise ordering, even if it were deemed desirable, without conducting a pre-trial at least as elaborate as the experiment itself. For example, a problem whose solution is simple $4C$ probably presents less difficulty than one involving steps leading to a more complicated expression such as $B + 2C - A$ or even $B + C - A$. Note that this may be true even though the steps required may be more numerous to reach $4C$ than one of the more complex expressions.[1] To state the matter differently, the number of steps involved to reach a solution is not precisely related to logical (or rather, psychological) difficulty. It is interesting in this connection to

---

[1]Actually, subjects had a great deal of difficulty with a problem whose solution was $3C$, $C = 27$, probably due to the effect of *Einstellung* (set) investigated by Luchins (52) using these problems. Since *Einstellung* depends on experience with previous problems, ordering appears as a factor in determining difficulty.

observe, for example, that the statistical analysis seems to show that the subjects tended to experience greater "difficulty" in reaching a solution as the capacity of the jars was increased — a psychological rather than a logical distinction being involved here.

Another illustration of possible sources of disturbance to the intended ordering is provided by reference to a lack of uniqueness for the solutions to some problems. For example, for the set of jars $\{A = 37, B = 18, C = 3\}$ the solution $B - 2C$, or a requirement of 6, was chosen at random. This solution requires 5 steps, but the simpler solution $2C$ requires only 3. Since it took some time to discover the existence of these simpler problems toward the end of the test, the discovery was considered part of the learning process and no attempt was made to eliminate or reorder the problems on the basis of alternate solutions.[1]

4A.2. Sample Documents

This section of the appendix is included to give the reader a better idea of precisely what the subjects encountered in the experiment. It is also included in the hope that data on similar tests, which would be comparable to these will be of aid to other experimenters.

The foms are filled out as they would be given to a Group B subject who attained his budget of 5 on Test 1 and a Group $C\gamma$ student who attained a score of 2 on Test 1, and an $A\alpha$ subject and an $A\gamma$ subject who did not attain the Test 1 budget.

---

[1]Experience with the tests indicated that this would have been a virtually impossible task. Subjects discovered as many as six solutions to some of the problems including, in several cases, simpler solutions than the experimenter had discovered indicating that he, too, exhibited *Einstellung*.

Instructions

In each problem you have three water jars, A, B, and C, with different capacities. With these jars you are expected to measure out the required amount of water *without approximating*. You may fill any of the jars from a spigot, empty any of them into the sink, or fill one jar from another jar. After a jar is filled from the spigot it must be filled to capacity, and after a jar is emptied into the sink it must have no water in it. After one jar is filled from another, *either* the jar which has been filled must be filled to capacity, *or* the jar from which water is poured must have no water.

For each problem you will be given the jar capacities and the required amount. The required amount must be the *total amount* of water *in the three jars* at the end of the problem. You are to answer the problem by filling in the appropriate blanks. Use only one line for each step.

Sample Problem 1: Capacities in quarts; A = 3, B = 7, C = 2. Required 1 quart.

Contents

Step					A	B	C
1.	Fill A	Empty	Fill	from	3	0	0
2.	Fill	Empty	Fill C	from A	1	0	2
3.	Fill	Empty C	Fill	from	1	0	0

Clearly, this is not the only solution to this problem. One alternate would be: Fill B, fill A from B, empty A, fill A from B, empty A. Either solution would be correct. In more complex problems it may be desirable to keep count of the number of quarts in each jar in the space at the right, as shown. This is not necessary, and *only the filling-in of the blanks in the steps will be checked.* (The list of contents will *not* be checked.)

A more complicated sample problem is shown below.

Sample Problem 2: Capacities; A = 27, B = 31, C = 17. Required 18.

Contents

				A	B	C
Fill B	Empty	Fill	from		31	
Fill	Empty	Fill C	from B		14	17
Fill	Empty C	Fill	from		14	
Fill	Empty	Fill A	from B	14		
Fill B	Empty	Fill	from	14	31	
Fill	Empty	Fill A	from B	27	18	
Fill	Empty A	Fill	from		18	

Exhibit 4A.1. Instructions (all groups)

96

You will be given six tests of *equal difficulty*, each containing 15 water jar problems. You will have seven minutes for each test. You are to complete *as many problems as you can* in the seven minutes allowed. A *goal* will be set on each test by which your performance will be judged. If you attain the *goal* (that is, complete the required number of problems correctly) you will be rewarded; if you complete fewer problems than the *goal*, you will be penalized. The reward on the six tests will be that you will receive $1.00. If you do not attain your *goal* on any of the six tests, you must pay back $1.00 as your penalty.

You will be given $3.00 at the start of the experiment. Should you have no money left at the start of *any* test, *you can still earn the reward*, but you will not pay the penalty. *If you attain the goal on all six tests you will go home with $9.00.* If you do not attain the goal on any test *you lose nothing*.

Before beginning Test 1 [you will be asked some questions on cards that will be passed out to you and] you will receive additional information.* During a three-minute break between tests your performance will be evaluated with respect to the goals which have been set for you and the rewards and penalties will be administered. [You will then be given additional information and asked some more questions. The answers to these questions will *not* be used in the determination of the goals. When you have answered the questions, turn the card over on the table. Once you have turned the card over, you will not be allowed to change your answers.]

At the end of the experiment you will be asked to sign a receipt for the money you have earned. *If you do not complete the experiment [or do not answer all of the questions on the cards which have been passed out to you], you will not be allowed to take your earnings from the room.*

YOU MUST NOT REVEAL THE NATURE OF THE EXPERI-
MENT TO OTHERS WHO MAY PARTICIPATE AS SUBJECTS
THERE MUST BE NO COMMUNICATION BETWEEN SUB-
JECTS DURING THE EXPERIMENT

*The form shown is for β and γ subjects. The Group α had instructions with the portions in brackets deleted.

Exhibit 4A.1 (cont.). Instructions (all groups)

Test 2

Problem 1: A = 21, B = 43, C = 28. Required 15.

Jar Contents

Step					A	B	C
1.	Fill	Empty	Fill	from	....	....	....
2.	Fill	Empty	Fill	from	....	....	....
3.	Fill	Empty	Fill	from	....	....	....
4.	Fill	Empty	Fill	from	....	....	....
5.	Fill	Empty	Fill	from	....	....	....
6.	Fill	Empty	Fill	from	....	....	....
7.	Fill	Empty	Fill	from	....	....	....
8.	Fill	Empty	Fill	from	....	....	....
9.	Fill	Empty	Fill	from	....	....	....
10.	Fill	Empty	Fill	from	....	....	....

Problem 2: A = 31, B = 8, C = 41. Required 57.

Step | | | | | | |
--- | --- | --- | --- | --- | --- | --- | ---
1. | Fill .... | Empty .... | Fill .... | from .... | .... | .... | ....
2. | Fill .... | Empty .... | Fill .... | from .... | .... | .... | ....
3. | Fill .... | Empty .... | Fill .... | from .... | .... | .... | ....
4. | Fill .... | Empty .... | Fill .... | from .... | .... | .... | ....
5. | Fill .... | Empty .... | Fill .... | from .... | .... | .... | ....
6. | Fill .... | Empty .... | Fill .... | from .... | .... | .... | ....
7. | Fill .... | Empty .... | Fill .... | from .... | .... | .... | ....
8. | Fill .... | Empty .... | Fill .... | from .... | .... | .... | ....
9. | Fill .... | Empty .... | Fill .... | from .... | .... | .... | ....
10. | Fill .... | Empty .... | Fill .... | from .... | .... | .... | ....

Problem 3: A = 47, B = 30, C = 14. Required 42.

Step | | | | | | |
--- | --- | --- | --- | --- | --- | --- | ---
1. | Fill .... | Empty .... | Fill .... | from .... | .... | .... | ....
2. | Fill .... | Empty .... | Fill .... | from .... | .... | .... | ....
3. | Fill .... | Empty .... | Fill .... | from .... | .... | .... | ....
4. | Fill .... | Empty .... | Fill .... | from .... | .... | .... | ....
5. | Fill .... | Empty .... | Fill .... | from .... | .... | .... | ....
6. | Fill .... | Empty .... | Fill .... | from .... | .... | .... | ....
7. | Fill .... | Empty .... | Fill .... | from .... | .... | .... | ....
8. | Fill .... | Empty .... | Fill .... | from .... | .... | .... | ....
9. | Fill .... | Empty .... | Fill .... | from .... | .... | .... | ....
10. | Fill .... | Empty .... | Fill .... | from .... | .... | .... | ....

Exhibit 4A.2. Sample test (all groups)

Problem 4: A = 30, B = 27, C = 17. Required 40.

Step					Jar Contents A	B	C
1.	Fill	Empty	Fill	from	....	....	....
2.	Fill	Empty	Fill	from	....	....	....
3.	Fill	Empty	Fill	from	....	....	....
4.	Fill	Empty	Fill	from	....	....	....
5.	Fill	Empty	Fill	from	....	....	....
6.	Fill	Empty	Fill	from	....	....	....
7.	Fill	Empty	Fill	from	....	....	....
8.	Fill	Empty	Fill	from	....	....	....
9.	Fill	Empty	Fill	from	....	....	....
10.	Fill	Empty	Fill	from	....	....	....

Problem 5: A = 30, B = 27, C = 36. Required 33.

Step							
1.	Fill	Empty	Fill	from	....	....	....
2.	Fill	Empty	Fill	from	....	....	....
3.	Fill	Empty	Fill	from	....	....	....
4.	Fill	Empty	Fill	from	....	....	....
5.	Fill	Empty	Fill	from	....	....	....
6.	Fill	Empty	Fill	from	....	....	....
7.	Fill	Empty	Fill	from	....	....	....
8.	Fill	Empty	Fill	from	....	....	....
9.	Fill	Empty	Fill	from	....	....	....
10.	Fill	Empty	Fill	from	....	....	....

Problem 6: A = 11, B = 25, C = 24. Required 26.

Step							
1.	Fill	Empty	Fill	from	....	....	....
2.	Fill	Empty	Fill	from	....	....	....
3.	Fill	Empty	Fill	from	....	....	....
4.	Fill	Empty	Fill	from	....	....	....
5.	Fill	Empty	Fill	from	....	....	....
6.	Fill	Empty	Fill	from	....	....	....
7.	Fill	Empty	Fill	from	....	....	....
8.	Fill	Empty	Fill	from	....	....	....
9.	Fill	Empty	Fill	from	....	....	....
10.	Fill	Empty	Fill	from	....	....	....

Exhibit 4A.2 (cont.). Sample test (all groups)

Problem 7: A = 50, B = 49, C = 19. Required 18.

Step					A	B	C
1.	Fill	Empty	Fill	from	....	....	....
2.	Fill	Empty	Fill	from	....	....	....
3.	Fill	Empty	Fill	from	....	....	....
4.	Fill	Empty	Fill	from	....	....	....
5.	Fill	Empty	Fill	from	....	....	....
6.	Fill	Empty	Fill	from	....	....	....
7.	Fill	Empty	Fill	from	....	....	....
8.	Fill	Empty	Fill	from	....	....	....
9.	Fill	Empty	Fill	from	....	....	....
10.	Fill	Empty	Fill	from	....	....	....

Problem 8: A = 5, B = 45, C = 40. Required 85.

Step							
1.	Fill	Empty	Fill	from	....	....	....
2.	Fill	Empty	Fill	from	....	....	....
3.	Fill	Empty	Fill	from	....	....	....
4.	Fill	Empty	Fill	from	....	....	....
5.	Fill	Empty	Fill	from	....	....	....
6.	Fill	Empty	Fill	from	....	....	....
7.	Fill	Empty	Fill	from	....	....	....
8.	Fill	Empty	Fill	from	....	....	....
9.	Fill	Empty	Fill	from	....	....	....
10.	Fill	Empty	Fill	from	....	....	....

Problem 9: A = 43, B = 36, C = 23. Required 33.

Step							
1.	Fill	Empty	Fill	from	....	....	....
2.	Fill	Empty	Fill	from	....	....	....
3.	Fill	Empty	Fill	from	....	....	....
4.	Fill	Empty	Fill	from	....	....	....
5.	Fill	Empty	Fill	from	....	....	....
6.	Fill	Empty	Fill	from	....	....	....
7.	Fill	Empty	Fill	from	....	....	....
8.	Fill	Empty	Fill	from	....	....	....
9.	Fill	Empty	Fill	from	....	....	....
10.	Fill	Empty	Fill	from	....	....	....

Exhibit 4A.2 (cont.). Sample test (all groups)

Problem 10: A = 35, B = 18, C = 33. Required 34.

Step					A	B	C
1.	Fill	Empty	Fill	from	....	....	....
2.	Fill	Empty	Fill	from	....	....	....
3.	Fill	Empty	Fill	from	....	....	....
4.	Fill	Empty	Fill	from	....	....	....
5.	Fill	Empty	Fill	from	....	....	....
6.	Fill	Empty	Fill	from	....	....	....
7.	Fill	Empty	Fill	from	....	....	....
8.	Fill	Empty	Fill	from	....	....	....
9.	Fill	Empty	Fill	from	....	....	....
10.	Fill	Empty	Fill	from	....	....	....

Problem 11: A = 12, B = 1, C = 45. Required 48.

Step							
1.	Fill	Empty	Fill	from	....	....	....
2.	Fill	Empty	Fill	from	....	....	....
3.	Fill	Empty	Fill	from	....	....	....
4.	Fill	Empty	Fill	from	....	....	....
5.	Fill	Empty	Fill	from	....	....	....
6.	Fill	Empty	Fill	from	....	....	....
7.	Fill	Empty	Fill	from	....	....	....
8.	Fill	Empty	Fill	from	....	....	....
9.	Fill	Empty	Fill	from	....	....	....
10.	Fill	Empty	Fill	from	....	....	C

Problem 12: A = 2, B = 42, C = 40. Required 36.

Step							
1.	Fill	Empty	Fill	from	....	....	....
2.	Fill	Empty	Fill	from	....	....	....
3.	Fill	Empty	Fill	from	....	....	....
4.	Fill	Empty	Fill	from	....	....	....
5.	Fill	Empty	Fill	from	....	....	....
6.	Fill	Empty	Fill	from	....	....	....
7.	Fill	Empty	Fill	from	....	....	....
8.	Fill	Empty	Fill	from	....	....	....
9.	Fill	Empty	Fill	from	....	....	....
10.	Fill	Empty	Fill	from	....	....	....

Exhibit 4A.2 (cont.). Sample test (all groups)

Problem 13: A = 23, B = 48, C = 19. Required 76.

Step					A	B	C
1.	Fill	Empty	Fill	from	....	....	....
2.	Fill	Empty	Fill	from	....	....	....
3.	Fill	Empty	Fill	from	....	....	....
4.	Fill	Empty	Fill	from	....	....	....
5.	Fill	Empty	Fill	from	....	....	....
6.	Fill	Empty	Fill	from	....	....	....
7.	Fill	Empty	Fill	from	....	....	....
8.	Fill	Empty	Fill	from	....	....	....
9.	Fill	Empty	Fill	from	....	....	....
10.	Fill	Empty	Fill	from	....	....	....

Problem 14: A = 42, B = 22, C = 31. Required 40.

Step					A	B	C
1.	Fill	Empty	Fill	from	....	....	....
2.	Fill	Empty	Fill	from	....	....	....
3.	Fill	Empty	Fill	from	....	....	....
4.	Fill	Empty	Fill	from	....	....	....
5.	Fill	Empty	Fill	from	....	....	....
6.	Fill	Empty	Fill	from	....	....	....
7.	Fill	Empty	Fill	from	....	....	....
8.	Fill	Empty	Fill	from	....	....	....
9.	Fill	Empty	Fill	from	....	....	....
10.	Fill	Empty	Fill	from	....	....	....

Problem 15: A = 27, B = 9, C = 8. Required 1.

Step					A	B	C
1.	Fill	Empty	Fill	from	....	....	....
2.	Fill	Empty	Fill	from	....	....	....
3.	Fill	Empty	Fill	from	....	....	....
4.	Fill	Empty	Fill	from	....	....	....
5.	Fill	Empty	Fill	from	....	....	....
6.	Fill	Empty	Fill	from	....	....	....
7.	Fill	Empty	Fill	from	....	....	....
8.	Fill	Empty	Fill	from	....	....	....
9.	Fill	Empty	Fill	from	....	....	....
10.	Fill	Empty	Fill	from	....	....	....

Exhibit 4A.2 (cont.). Sample test (all groups)

Based on your experience on Test 1 and the knowledge that Test 1 and Test 2 are of equal difficulty, please answer the following questions.

How many problems do *you personally* hope to complete on Test 2? ....

Do you believe that you should be penalized if you do not complete as many problems as you hope to? ....
(yes or no)

If your answer to the last question was "no," at what level do you think *we* should set the goal for your performance? In other words, how many problems do you think *we should require* you to complete in order to receive the reward? ....

Exhibit 4A.3. Sample aspiration level determination questionnaire (Group β)

The goal has been set by which your performance on Test 2 will be judged. If you solve the goal number of problems or more correctly, you will receive $1.00. If you solve fewer problems than the goal you must pay back $1.00. You will not be told what this goal is. Work as hard as you can on this test.

Exhibit 4A.4. Sample budget (Groups Aα, Bα)

The goal by which your performance on Test 2 will be judged is 6 problems. If you solve this number of problems or more correctly, you will receive $1.00. If you complete fewer problems than the goal, you must pay back $1.00.

Exhibit 4A.5. Sample budget (Groups Bα, Cα, Dα, Bβ, Cβ, Dβ)

The goal by which your performance on Test 2 will be judged is 4 problems. If you solve that number of problems or more correctly, you will receive $1.00. If you complete fewer problems than the goal, you must pay back $1.00.

Based on your experience on Test 1 and the knowledge that Test 1 and Test 2 are of equal difficulty, please answer the following questions.

How many problems do *you personally* hope to complete on Test 2? ....

Do you believe that you should be penalized if you do not complete as many problems as you hope to? ....
(yes or no)

If your answer to the last question was "no," at what level do you think *we* should set the goal for your performance? In other words, how many problems do you think *we should require* you to complete in order to receive the reward? ....

Exhibit 4A.6. Sample budget — aspiration level combination (Groups Bγ, Cγ, Dγ)

A goal has been set by which your performance on Test 2 will be judged. If you solve the goal number of problems or more correctly, you will receive $1.00. If you solve fewer problems than the goal, you must pay back $1.00. You will not be told what the goal is, but what do you guess that it is? .... (Specify number of problems.) Work as hard as you can on this test.

Based on your previous experience, knowing that Test 2 is equal in difficulty to the previous tests, please answer the following questions.

How many problems do *you personally* hope to complete on Test 2? ....

Do you believe that you should be penalized if you do not complete as many problems as you hope to?

(yes or no)

If your answer to the last question was "no," at what level do you think *we* should set the goal for your performance? In other words, how many problems do you think *we should require* you to complete in order to receive the reward? ....

Exhibit 4A.7. Sample budget — aspiration level combination (Group Aγ)

Name_____

We would like to find out some of your reactions to the experiment. Please feel free to answer these questions candidly, and as fully as you like.

Did you enjoy participating in the experiment? .... Why or why not?
....
....

Did you feel a sense of competition with the other participants, or were you really competing only against yourself?
....

Did the money rewards make you try harder? ....

Would you have worked harder if the money rewards were higher — say $2.00 per test throughout? ....

Do you think the goals were: (a) too low; (b) just about right; or (c) too high for judging your performance? ....
(a, b, or c)

Were you satisfied with your performance on the experiment? ....
....
....

Did you feel that you were working toward a goal that you had set up for yourself or one that we had set for you? Explain: ....
....
....
....

Did you feel tense at any time during the experiment? ....

How do you think the budgets* were set? ....
....

Write down any comments you wish about the conduct of the experiment, or your own attitudes toward it.

*"Goals" should have been used instead of "budgets" in this question.

Exhibit 4A.8. Sample questionnaire

How did you interpret the question, "How many problems do you personally hope to complete?"..

....

....

....

Did you find that there was much difference between that question and the one which asked about the number of problems we should require you to complete? ....

....

....

Exhibit 4A.8 (cont.). Sample questionnaire

Groups β and γ only

TABLE 4A.2. CLASSIFICATION OF SUBJECTS IN EXPERIMENTAL GROUPING

	Industrial Management			Industrial Administration		Engineering		Aggregate "Years of Study"
	Soph.	Jr.	Sr.	1st yr.	2nd yr.	Sr.	Adv. Grad.	
Aα	5		1		3			32
Aβ	1	1		4		3		37
Aγ		2	3	4				38
Bα	4		1		4			36
Bβ				5		4		41
Bγ		2	3	3			1	39
Cα	4				4		1	38
Cβ	1			4		4		38
Cγ		2	2	3		2		37
Dα	4				3		2	38
Dβ	1			5		3		39
Dγ		3	2	3			1	38
Totals	20	10	12	31	14	16	5	

APPENDIX 4B ADDITIONAL STATISTICAL RESULTS

TABLE 4B.1. NUMBER OF PROBLEMS SOLVED ON EACH TEST BY EACH GROUP OF NINE SUBJECTS

| Aspiration | α — Budget only | | | | | | | β — (1) Aspiration (2) Budget | | | | | | | γ — (1) Budget (2) Aspiration | | | | | | |
Budget \ Test	1	2	3	4	5	6	Total α	1	2	3	4	5	6	Total β	1	2	3	4	5	6	Total γ
A (implicit)	30	39	31	35	40	71	246	30	44	42	44	52	80	292	29	44	47	40	57	85	302
B (low)	27	28	38	32	37	59	221	25	38	38	37	45	71	254	27	37	38	33	43	68	246
C (medium)	32	39	29	34	35	66	235	30	49	50	34	50	81	294	33	49	44	40	52	79	297
D (high)	29	44	40	35	44	85	277	24	36	34	32	37	55	218	36	48	52	43	54	83	316
	118	150	138	136	156	281	979	109	167	164	147	184	287	1058	125	178	181	156	206	315	1161

TABLE 4B.2. NUMBER OF PROBLEMS SOLVED ON EACH TEST BY EACH BUDGET GROUP

Budget \ Test	1	2	3	4	5	6	All Tests
A	89	127	120	119	149	236	840
B	79	103	114	102	125	198	721
C	95	137	123	108	137	226	826
D	89	128	126	110	135	223	811
All Budgets	352	495	483	439	546	883	3198

TABLE 4B.3. PERFORMANCE.   PROBABILITY OF SIGNIFICANT DIFFERENCE
BETWEEN ASPIRATION LEVEL GROUPS

Group	β	γ
α	.981	1.000*
β		.998

*To 3 decimal places.

TABLE 4B.4.   PERFORMANCE.   PROBABILITY OF SIGNIFICANT DIFFERENCE
BETWEEN BUDGET GROUPS

	B	C	D
A	1.000*	.369	.680
B		1.000*	.998
C			.393

*To 3 decimal places.

TABLE 4B.5.   PERFORMANCE.   PROBABILITY OF SIGNIFICANT DIFFERENCE
BETWEEN NINE-MAN GROUPS

(Determined by two-tailed t-test with 106 degrees of freedom)

Total →		277	254	246	246	235	221	218
Score ↓	Group → ↓	$D\alpha$	$B\beta$	$B\gamma$	$A\alpha$	$C\alpha$	$B\alpha$	$D\beta$
316	$D\gamma$	*	†	†	†	†	†	†
302	$A\gamma$		*	*	*	†	†	†
297	$C\gamma$		x	*	*	†	†	†
294	$C\beta$		x	*	*	†	†	†
292	$A\beta$		x	*	*	†	†	†
277	$D\alpha$					x	*	†
254	$B\beta$							x

Symbol   †   *   x
Significance Level   .1%   1%   5%

108

Due to:	Sum of Squares	DF	Mean Square	Variance Ratio	
Main Effects:					
Linear t	1010.542	1	1010.542	193.702	†
Quadratic t	230.480	1	230.480	44.179	†
Cubic t	314.850	1	314.850	60.351	†
R = quartic + t	1.628	2	1.628	.310	
Total t	1557.500	5			
a	77.121	2	38.561	77.391	†
b	53.315	3	17.772	3.406	*
Interactions (2-way)					
$a \times$ linear t	6.291	2	3.146	.603	
$a \times$ quadratic t	7.251	2	3.626	.695	
$a \times$ cubic t	.458	2	.229	.044	
$R = a \times$ quartic + t	8.324	4	2.801	.536	
Total (ta)	22.324	10			
$b \times$ linear t	8.731	3	2.910	.557	
$b \times$ quadratic t	3.451	3	1.150	.220	
$b \times$ cubic t	6.507	3	2.169	.416	
$R = b \times$ quartic + t	3.039	6	.506	.097	
Total (tb)	21.728	15			
(ab)	100.323	6	16.721	3.205	†
Interactions (3-way)					
(ab) $\times$ linear t	23.807	5	4.761	.911	
(ab) $\times$ quadratic t	6.995	5	1.399	.268	
(ab) $\times$ cubic t	13.737	5	2.747	.526	
R = (ab) $\times$ quartic + t	19.317	10	1.932	.370	
Total (tab)	63.856	30			
Error	3005.111	576	5.217		
Total	4901.278	647			

t = test R = remainder
a = aspiration   *denotes significance at 5% level
b = budget   †denotes significance at 1% level

TABLE 4B.7.   ANALYSIS OF VARIANCE — PERFORMANCE ON INDIVIDUAL TESTS

| All Tests | | Test 1 | | | Test 2 | | | Test 3 | | |
Due to	DF	Sum of Squares	Mean Square	Variance Ratio	Sum of Squares	Mean Square	Variance Ratio	Sum of Squares	Mean Square	Variance Ratio
Main Effects										
Aspiration Levels (a)	2	3.574	1.787	.744	11.056	5.528	.938	26.056	13.028	3.569*
Budgets (b)	3	4.889	1.630	.678	23.509	7.836	1.329	2.917	.972	.266
Interaction Aspirations × Budgets (ab)	6	5.389	.898	.372	13.241	2.207	.375	33.500	5.583	1.529
Error (Remainder)	96	230.889	2.405	—	566.444	5.900	—	350.444	3.650	—
Total	107	244.471	—	—	614.250	—	—	412.917	—	—

*denotes significance at 5% level.

TABLE 4B.7 (cont.). ANALYSIS OF VARIANCE — PERFORMANCE ON INDIVIDUAL TESTS

All Tests		Test 4			Test 5			Test 6		
Due to	DF	Sum of Squares	Mean Square	Variance Ratio	Sum of Squares	Mean Square	Variance Ratio	Sum of Squares	Mean Square	Variance Ratio
Main Effects										
Aspiration Levels (a)	2	5.574	2.787	.461	34.889	17.445	3.800*	18.296	9.148	1.051
Budgets (b)	3	5.509	1.836	.305	10.778	3.593	.783	28.990	9.663	1.110
Interaction Aspirations × Budgets (ab)	6	10.352	1.725	.285	21.333	3.556	.775	78.815	13.136	1.509
Error (Remainder)	96	581.111	6.053	—	440.667	4.590	—	835.556	8.704	—
Total	107	602.546	—	—	507.667	—	—	961.657	—	—

*denotes significance at 5% level.

111

Due to	Sum of Squares	DF	Mean Square	Variance Ratio
Main Effects				
Tests (t)	57.611	4	14.403	2.285
Aspiration				
Levels (a)	4.225	1	4.225	.669
Budgets (b)	117.142	3	39.047	6.194††
Interactions (2-way)				
Tests $\times$				
Aspirations (ta)	9.845	4	2.461	.390
Tests $\times$				
Budgets (tb)	42.455	12	3.538	.561
Aspirations $\times$				
Budgets (ab)	29.897	3	9.966	1.581
Interactions (3-way)				
Tests $\times$				
Aspirations $\times$	649.623	12	54.135	8.587††
Budgets (tab)				
Error				
(Remainder)	2017.222	320	6.304	—
Total	2326.375	359	—	—

††denotes significance at .1% level.

Due to	Sum of Squares	DF	Mean Square	Variance Ratio
Main Effects:				
Tests (t)	591.128	4	147.782	17.790††
Aspiration				
Levels (a)	7.226	1	7.226	.870
Budgets (b)	122.075	3	40.692	4.899†
Interactions (2-way)				
Tests $\times$				
Aspirations (ta)	2.316	4	.579	.070
Tests $\times$				
Budgets (tb)	50.605	12	4.217	.508
Aspirations $\times$	50.674	3	16.891	2.033
Budgets (ab)				
Interactions (3-way)				
Tests $\times$				
Aspirations $\times$	64.754	12	5.396	.650
Budgets (tab)				
Error				
(Remainder)	2658.222	320	8.307	—
Total	3520.864	359	—	—

†denotes significance at 1% level.
††denotes significance at .1% level.

CHAPTER 5

A Mathematical Model for
Budgetary Planning

5.1. Introduction

To this point in the thesis the emphasis — both experimental and analytical — has centered on individual performance. Qualifications were introduced from time to time in order to draw attention to other problems relevant to budgetary management. One such problem involves issues of coordination between departments, a problem of particular importance insofar as behavior in one department may affect (favorably or adversely) the conditions of operation in another. Where such relations — called "factor cooperancy"[1] and "rivalry" in technical

---

[1]The term "factor" of production should be emphasized, because the economic theory of production is based on a model of the firm which distinguishes only between an entrepreneur (at the top) who makes all "basic" decisions, and factors of production, (labor and capital) that follow to the result intended by the entrepreneur. In particular, this theory does not allow for intervening tiers of management — distinguished as planning, operating, and control agents by W. W. Cooper (20) — and the kinds of immediate or ultimate consequences such intervention may have for any particular firm. It follows that there is no problem other than that of resource allocation (which occurs only along a technological optimum) and, in particular, there is no problem of control — e.g., aspiration levels of intermediaries, report content (or timing), etc. (Cf., e.g., H. Guetzkow and H. A. Simon (71) for an experimental study which shows that the realization of an optimum depends, at least in part, on the kinds of information, organization arrangements, etc., supplied to participants.) However, the basic categorizations such as efficiency (defined in alternative cost terms), marginalism (broadly conceived), cooperancy, rivalry, etc., do carry over as useful constructs at a more fundamental level, and the current economic model of the firm should therefore not be allowed to stand in the way of the use of these concepts merely because of inadequacies in the vehicle used for their transmission.

economics — are present, it then follows, as is well known from economic theory, that optimization undertaken department by department does not guarantee an overall optimum.[1]

It is clear that pursuit of the techniques advanced in earlier chapters could at best produce rules for obtaining the optimum in each department taken separately. A simple example will suffice to show that the definition of an optimum for a single department cannot be made *in vacuo*. Recognizing the rather obvious interdependency of cost and rate of production, should the decision be to increase production at an optimum rate in a given department, to keep unit cost constant, or to reduce cost at an optimum rate while keeping production constant? This question cannot, of course, be answered with the aid of the control mechanisms discussed earlier. Expressed in other terms, the perfection of techniques for controlling the unicellular organism is a futile undertaking (from the point of view of budget control if not that of psychology) unless some means of establishing subgoals for each of the controlled units based on the overall aims of the entity can be developed.

It is the purpose of this chapter to explore this topic in some depth. This will be done by means of the techniques of linear programming which appear to be the most suitable of the available analytic methods for this purpose. A particular model will be synthesized which has the following advantages: (a) it exhibits the desired features in a simple and straightforward manner; and (b), because of its special structure, admits the possibility of evolving especially efficient methods of solution.[2]

Although the study to be conducted in this chapter has its most obvious relevance in the area of planning,[3] it also has rather clear

---

[1]An overall optimum would then be secured only in the case of "independence" (as distinguished from rivalry and cooperancy). Cf. Sune Carlson (5).

Incidentally there are further possibilities that require attention such as "optima in the small" and "optima in the large." These need not be dealt with here, however, since linear programming, when applicable, guarantees the emergence of the latter. See, e.g., A. Charnes, W. W. Cooper, and A. Henderson (15).

[2]*Vide*, A. Charnes and W. W. Cooper, "Management Models and Industrial Applications of Linear Programming," *Management Science* (10), where the import of such special model types is discussed for its future bearing on (a) application and (b) scientific research.

[3]In the sense of choosing between alternatives when, as is generally true in economics, no issue of follow-up or implementation is involved so that no problem of control is involved. Examples of this kind are the pricing delegation studies to be found in T. C. Koopmans (45c) or A. Charnes and W. W. Cooper (14). The latter, it should be noted, does discuss the possibility of control problems emerging (e.g., in their discussion of contradictory systems), and the point is even more strongly

implications for the kind of budgetary control problems which are of interest for this thesis. Thus, as indicated above, a crucial issue which may emerge is the specification of rules for guiding or stimulating departmental behavior in certain directions in order to achieve certain overall results. For instance, a question may be asked whether costs (including transfer costs and prices) should be reported accurately, and be based on fair and equitable procedures. Or is it better — e.g., in achieving an overall optimum — to adopt an alternate approach and report costs to each supervisor which, though distorted from the stand-point of the overall entity, nevertheless succeed in furthering entity objectives? Finally, if either approach be adopted, how fair (or unfair) or how accurate (or inaccurate) should the reports be?

While these topics cannot be fully explored here, and while experimental (or empirical) evidence of a kind that might be desired is not yet available, there is some advantage in conducting preliminary analytic explorations. Minimally, it should then be possible, at least in principle, to explore some implications of various costing, reporting, and budgeting rules that are of interest because of their potential relevance for currently employed methods in practice.

Such an exploration, then, constitutes the main objective of this chapter. The task will be regarded as complete when main issues have been clarified, and no effort will be made (as in the preceding chapters) to carry things forward to a resolution which, in the end, must depend on some measure of empirical verification. In the process of clarification an effort will be made to provide details for synthesizing certain kinds of models and to supply prescriptions for a procedure of solution that will, at least in some situations, provide a beginning for applying the results of the inquiry which is to be conducted.

5.2. The Hierarchy of the Factors of Production

The management science literature has dealt largely with problems in which the strategic factors[1] are a priori determined. For example, in the machine loading problem the amount of each output is determined solely from the costs and limitations associated with the set of factors

---

hinted at by Charnes and Cooper (10) when the possible desirability of supplying "misinformation" to subordinates is noted. Also of interest in this connection are studies which deal with decision-making by teams, such as by J. Marschak (58) and R. Radner (63a).

[1]For a discussion of the specific meaning of strategic factor as it is used here, see Barnard (3).

"machine hours."[1] An implicit assumption in a model of this type is that the costs of other factors of production are either negligible or are proportional to the amount of machine-hour usage or output. Furthermore, it is necessary that availability restrictions on other factors are redundant — i.e., that the set of things known as "machine hours" is a strategic factor. To put the matter another way, the felicity of any such model depends vitally on whether or not it incorporates all of the relevant bottlenecks relative to the criteria which are of interest as stated (or as they should be stated) in the objective function.

In order to carry this analysis a step further, assume that there is a machine manager who administers the operation of the several machines. From his vantage point, when he "solves" the machine loading problem (i.e., maximizes profit or minimizes cost subject to certain output requirements and restrictions) he will discover, within the strategic factors, limits on the capacity of one or more machines (or their operators).

If the assumption that "machine hours" is *the* strategic factor is removed, it is fairly easy to visualize a labor manager and a materials manager on the same level of the hierarchy as the machine manager.[2] As viewed from the vantage point of the department head to whom these three report, the operations of any or all of the machine managers may be looked upon as a strategic factor. Proceeding an additional level up the organizational ladder, the supervisor to whom this department head and several others report can either view each department as a single factor; or he can investigate a level deeper, considering as factors labor, materials, machine hours (and even managers at much lower tiers) in each department.

In the discussion that follows, it will be assumed that each supervisor can "see" two levels below him. In this sense an attempt will be made to focus on features of what Charnes and Cooper (10) call a "hierarchial model."

5.3. The Concept of Limited Substitution — A Definition

The production functions of economics have certain drawbacks

---

[1] See, for example, Cooper and Charnes (10), pp. 48-57; and for another example in the scheduling of an oil refinery, Manne (56) deals with crude oil availability as a limiting factor.

[2] It is not actually necessary that there be a "machine-hour manager" as such; it is equally possible to consider these managers as "chunks" of supervisory time, time in which the department head spends in managing these factors, as opposed to time spent in supervising the managers. Clearly, at some level in an organization a point will be reached where a man is managing *things* rather than *people*. It is expected that this will be true at the lowest level (i.e., production workers), partially true at the next higher level, etc.

including lack of empirical validation on the one hand and of easy access to managerial data (or even ways of thinking) on the other hand. This suggests that the topic at issue may best be formulated in some other manner, if possible, since there is little advantage to piling one difficulty upon another when empirical validation is ultimately undertaken. The approach (e.g., via linear programming) that has been common in management science has a certain appeal. But as pointed out above, the efforts here have (to date) been restricted to isolating one set of strategic factors and to concentrating only upon the factors thus isolated in a way which may best be described as focusing on one level of management. Such an approach has limitations which become apparent in cases such as those where an a priori choice of strategic factors is not obvious. Of course, if the problem is sufficiently simple the limitational factors may be verified, perhaps easily, in one form or another by direct observation; in larger problems parameterization techniques may be used to secure required guidance. But in many situations it may not be possible to depend on either of these modes of validation, and other possibilities may then need to be considered. In particular, it may become necessary to consider the synthesis of procedures which will raise alarms or danger signals when one strategic factor or another has been omitted from the model (explicit or implicit) used to plan the activities that will be undertaken. Another case of interest that arises is one which will be called "limited substitution." Here the use of mutually exclusive categories, which is assumed, may be misleading, especially in a linear model; nevertheless, it is assumed that, under certain conditions, it is possible to effect substitutions (or at least limited substitutions) *within* the original groupings.[1]

5.4. Form of the Production Function Under Limited Substitution[2]

It is readily seen that the assumptions of limited substitution lead immediately to a production function in which the output of each item

---

[1]These involve issues of aggregation and model detail which cannot be discussed here at any length, aside from the obvious comments already entered. That the issue of "linearity" is involved can be seen from the fact that the indicated substitutions — at some specified level of aggregation — would make their effects felt via the coefficients (which then become functions of the outputs and mixes).

[2]The limited substitution model presented here was developed independently by the author and reported in (76). I was given access to the unpublished paper by Charnes, Cooper, and Miller (18) after the formulation was completed. The model, although a special case of their general dyadic formulation, is not specifically described in that paper, and, in any case, the computation scheme stands as an original development in its own right.

is limited to the amount (in terms of product-equivalents) of the factors that will be allocated to its production within each factor subgroup. Under optimization the choice is designated to the factor subgroup which "costs" the least. Determinacy, on the other hand, requires that at least one such factor subgroup be strategic, since otherwise no limit to expansion would be present.

In addition to assuming that at least one strategic subgroup exists, it is further assumed that the substitution within groups is linear. The limitation on the output of any item may then be expressed as a set of linear inequalities where the number of inequations is equal to the number of factor subgroups from which inputs are required for this particular item.

For the model to be considered, let there be p factor subgroups, and let it be supposed that the ith item requires inputs from q_i of the subgroups. Further, let

x'_{ijk} = number of units of the kth factor of the jth subgroup used in production of the ith product[1]

(5.4.1) a_{ijk} = number of product equivalents of the ith item produced per unit of x'_{ijk}

y_i = amount of the ith item produced

n_j = number of factors in the jth subgroup

The condition to be imposed on the ith item may then be written[2]

$$(5.4.2) \qquad\qquad y_i \leq \sum_{j \epsilon q_i} \sum_{k=1}^{n_j} a_{ijk} x'_{ijk} \qquad\qquad i = 1, \ldots, m$$

---

[1]The reason for the use of primes on x and c will become evident in equations 5.4.7 where the transformation performed on these variables is shown.

[2]If only a subset of the n_j factors is used in producing the ith item, then for those nonutilized factors, it is assumed that

$$a_{ijk} = 1$$

$$c'_{ijk} = M$$

where, as usual, M is a large penalty associated with an artificial process whose cost is therefore so high that it will not appear at an optimum when solutions exist. See (10), p. 50. Where nonutilized subsets are known in advance they may, of course, be eliminated from consideration at the outset. The device suggested here is intended for ex post facto adjustments where, after an initial optimum has been achieved, it is found desirable to "derive" some of the factors out of positive use.

Noting that the factor subgroups are mutually exclusive, the factor availabilities may be written:

$$(5.4.3) \qquad \sum_{i=1}^{m} x'_{ijk} \leq b_{jk}$$

where b_{jk} is the maximum amount available of the jth subgroup in the kth factor grouping. This restriction states that the total amount of factors, considered over all products, cannot exceed a prescribed number, b_{jk} for $k = 1, \ldots, n_j; j = 1, \ldots, p$, so that

$$(5.4.3a) \qquad \sum_{j=1}^{p} \sum_{i=1}^{m} x'_{ijk} \leq \sum_{j=1}^{p} b_{jk} = b_k$$

and

$$(5.4.3b) \qquad \sum_{k=1}^{nj} \sum_{i=1}^{m} x'_{ijk} \leq \sum_{k=1}^{nj} b_{jk} = b_j$$

In other words neither the amount, b_k, of any factor group or the amount, b_j, of any subgroup can be exceeded either in any or all of the activities to be undertaken.

The problem is to maximize the difference between the contribution of the outputs and the costs of the necessary inputs.

Let

$$(5.4.4)$$

$c_i = $ the contribution per unit of the ith item to profit and overhead

$c'_{ijk} = $ cost of one unit of x'_{ijk}

An analytical expression of the function to be maximized is therefore

$$(5.4.5) \qquad \sum_{i=1}^{m} \left(c_i y_i - \sum_{j \, eq \, i} \sum_{k=1}^{nj} c'_{ijk} x'_{ijk} \right)$$

and the maximization is to be undertaken over the previously stated constraints and is also to take into consideration restrictions of the form (which may emanate from inventory and sales considerations)

$$(5.4.6) \qquad L_i \leq y_i \leq U_i$$

This last restriction is in what is called bounded variables form which, as Charnes and Lemke (16) note, is typical of many management problems involving "balance restrictions."[1]

---

[1]Thus the L_i and U_i may be, say, lower and upper limits to inventory, or else they may emanate from the need for supplying certain minimal (and not more than maximal) amounts to certain markets.

It is now assumed — although this is not essential — that the number of factors exceeds the number of products. For convenience it is now also desirable to introduce certain transformations which "normalize" or express the production restrictions in terms of "unit" amounts. For this purpose, let

$$x_{ijk} = x'_{ijk} \, a_{ijk}$$

(5.4.7)
$$b_{ijk} = \frac{1}{a_{ijk}}$$

$$c_{ijk} = \frac{c'_{ijk}}{a_{ijk}}$$

Using (5.4.7), factor usage can be expressed in units of product equivalents of the outputs for which they are used. If the c_{ijk}'s and a_{ijk}'s are positive and no lower bound (other than those emanating from the constraints and non-negativity) is placed on the x'_{ijk}'s, the inequality in (5.4.2) can, for purposes of optimization, be replaced by equality, since it will never be most profitable to utilize a combination of factors which will satisfy any of these constraints as a strict inequality. The problem may thus state in the following final form

Maximize:

$$\sum_{i=1}^{m} \left(c_i y_i - \sum_{j \epsilon q_i} \sum_{k=1}^{n_j} c_{ijk} \, x_{ijk} \right)$$

Subject to

$$\sum_{k=1}^{n_j} x_{ijk} - y_i = 0 \qquad\qquad i = 1, \dots, m; \; j\epsilon q_i$$

(5.4.8)
$$\sum_{i=1}^{m} b_{ijk} x_{ijk} \leq b_{jk} \qquad\qquad k = 1, \dots, n_j; \; j\epsilon q_i$$

$$y_i \leq U_i \qquad\qquad i = 1, \dots, m$$

$$-y_i \leq -L_i$$

The dual to the above problem is[1]

Minimize:

$$\sum_{j=1}^{p} \sum_{k=1}^{n_j} b_{jk} K_{jk} + \sum_{i=1}^{m} \tau_i U_i - \sum_{i=1}^{m} \beta_i L_i$$

---

[1]Following the notation for the dual variables used in Danzig's row-column sum method of solution of the transportation model described in (45a).

Subject to

$$R_{ij} + b_{ijk}K_{jk} \geq -c_{ijk} \qquad i = 1, ..., m;\; j\epsilon q_i$$

(5.4.9)
$$k = 1, ..., n_j$$

$$-\sum_{j\epsilon q_i} R_{ij} + \tau_i - \beta_i \geq c_i \qquad i = 1, ..., m$$

$K_{jk}, \tau_i, \beta_i \geq 0$ and R_{ij} is unrestricted in sign.

The theorem of the alternative in linear program asserts that strict inequality cannot, at an optimum, simultaneously obtain for (1) a dual variable and the corresponding direct constraint or (2) a direct variable and its associated dual constraint.[1]

From (1) it is clear that, at optimum, $\tau_i > 0$ implies $y_i = U_i$ and $\beta_i > 0$ implies $y_i = L_i$.[2] Furthermore, $y_i < U_i$ implies $\tau_i = 0$ and $L_i < y_i$ implies $\beta_i = 0$. Therefore, utilizing (2) and assuming the nonexistence of degeneracy[3] the conditions for optimality are

$$R_{ij} + b_{ijk}\; K_{jk} = -c_{ijk} \quad x_{ijk} > 0$$

$$\geq -c_{ijk} \quad \text{elsewhere}$$

$$\sum_{j\epsilon q_i} R_{ij} = c_i \quad L_i < y_i > U_i$$

(5.4.10)
$$-\sum_{j\epsilon q_i} R_{ij} < c_i \quad y_i = U_i$$

$$-\sum_{j\epsilon q_i} R_{ij} > c_i \quad y_i = L_i$$

5.5. Example of a Limited Substitution Problem

For exposition purposes a model has been chosen which utilizes three factor groups to be called "labor," "materials," and "machine hours." Three products will be produced. Products 1 and 2 require inputs from all three factor groups, but Product 3 is a hand operation, requiring labor and materials only. There are three types of labor, two types of material, and four types of machines.

The restrictions of the model are presented in simplex form in Figure 5.1 in order to bring out the details of model structure by reference to a standard format used in this field of analysis. Structurally (i.e., without regard to numerical magnitudes of the coefficients) the resemblance to a transportation model is striking. If, in fact, complete substitution

---

[1] *Vide* (81).

[2] For a more complete treatment of the bounded variables problem, see (13) or (16).

[3] *Vide* (9) for methods of resolving degeneracy.

	P_0	Equality or Inequality	Product 1 Labor	Product 1 Mtl.	Product 1 Mach. Hr.	Product 2 Labor	Product 2 Mtl.	Product 2 Mach. Hr.	Product 3 Labor	Product 3 Mtl.	y_1	y_2	y_3	Dual Variables
Production Function	0	$=$	$1\ 1\ 1$								-1			R_{11}
	0	$=$		$1\ 1$							-1			R_{12}
	0	$=$			$1\ 1\ 1\ 1$						-1			R_{13}
	0	$=$				$1\ 1\ 1$						-1		R_{21}
	0	$=$					$1\ 1$					-1		R_{22}
	0	$=$						$1\ 1\ 1\ 1$				-1		R_{23}
	0	$=$							$1\ 1\ 1$				-1	R_{31}
	0	$=$								$1\ 1$			-1	R_{32}
Factor Availabilities	b_{11}	$\leq$	$b_{111}\ b_{112}\ b_{113}$											K_{11}
	b_{12}	$\leq$		$b_{121}\ b_{122}$										K_{12}
	b_{13}	$\leq$			$b_{131}\ b_{132}\ b_{133}\ b_{134}$									K_{13}
	b_{21}	$\leq$				$b_{211}\ b_{212}\ b_{213}$								K_{21}
	b_{22}	$\leq$					$b_{221}\ b_{222}$							K_{22}
	b_{31}	$\leq$						$b_{231}\ b_{232}\ b_{233}\ b_{234}$						K_{31}
	b_{32}	$\leq$							$b_{311}\ b_{312}\ b_{313}$					K_{32}
	b_{33}	$\leq$								$b_{321}\ b_{322}$				K_{33}
	b_{34}	$\leq$												K_{34}
Output Bounds — Upper	U_1	$\leq$									1			τ_1
	U_2	$\leq$										1		τ_2
	U_3	$\leq$											1	τ_3
Output Bounds — Lower	$-L_1$	$\leq$									-1			β_1
	$-L_2$	$\leq$										-1		β_2
	$-L_3$	$\leq$											-1	β_3

Fig. 5.1. Production under limited substitution — simplex tableau form

between groups existed, the tableau could be compressed into a transportation schema by suitably arranged scalings. However, a special (and more efficient) computational scheme may be synthesized from the prescriptions for "sub-dual algorithms" as set forth in Charnes, Cooper, and Miller (18).[1]

$$
\begin{aligned}
\text{Labor} \quad & y_1 = \tfrac{1}{5}x'_{111} + \tfrac{1}{4}x'_{112} + \tfrac{1}{3}x'_{113} \\
\text{Material} \quad & y_1 = \tfrac{1}{5}x'_{121} + \tfrac{1}{4}x'_{122} \\
\text{Machine Hrs.} \quad & y_1 = 1.2x'_{131} + 1x'_{132} + 1x'_{133} + .8x'_{134} \\
\text{Labor} \quad & y_2 = \tfrac{1}{2}x'_{211} + \tfrac{1}{2}x'_{212} + \tfrac{1}{2}x'_{213} \\
\text{Material} \quad & y_2 = \tfrac{1}{2}x'_{221} + \tfrac{1}{3}x'_{222} \\
\text{Machine Hrs.} \quad & y_2 = 1.8x'_{231} + 1.2x'_{232} + 1x'_{233} + .5x'_{234} \\
\text{Labor} \quad & y_3 = \tfrac{1}{10}x'_{312} + \tfrac{1}{6}x'_{313} \\
\text{Material} \quad & y_3 = 1x'_{321} + 1x'_{322}
\end{aligned}
$$

(5.5.1)

It is seen that a unit of Product 1 may be produced using 5 units of the first type of labor, 4 of the second type, or 3 of the third. But a unit of product *also* requires either 5 units of the first type of material or 4 units of the second, and similarly requires 1/1.2 units of machine type 1 time, 1 hour of machine type 2, 1 of type 3, or 1/.8 of type 4; similarly for products 2 and 3. It should be noted that Product 3 is "short-changed." It requires no machine time, but also cannot use labor type 1 which (as shown below) is the cheapest labor source. It might be surmised that Product 3 is produced by a reasonably-skilled hand operation which requires labor which is more skilled than type 1 and is seen to be more "sensitive" to the increase in skill between labor types 2 and 3 than either of Products 1 and 2.

It should be re-emphasized here that the production restrictions might have been stated in the form of inequalities — e.g., y_i requires at least so much labor — but as the c_{ijk}'s that will be used are positive, and no lower bounds are placed on factor usage,[2] no slack would exist

---

[1]It may be noted, however, that the instructions supplied in this article are of an extremely general character and will probably remain so until, as these authors note, an "algorithm for generating algorithms [including requisite models and transformations] have been completely prescribed." In short, it is by no means certain in which direction to proceed from these general instructions.

[2]It is reasonable to believe that for "worker morale" or other long-term consideration, lower bounds might be placed on labor. This can be arranged by treating labor slack as a bounded variable, but is avoided here to prevent increasing the complexity of the exposition.

at optimum; therefore, as previously noted, an equivalent equality may be used instead.

The product contributions per unit of output and factor costs per unit of input are shown in Figure 5.2.

Factor Group	Labor			Material		Machine Hours			
Factor Type	1	2	3	1	2	1	2	3	4
Symbol	c'_{i11}	c'_{i12}	c'_{i13}	c'_{i21}	c'_{i22}	c'_{i31}	c'_{i32}	c'_{i33}	c'_{i34}
Unit Cost (\$)	1.8	2	2.5	4	3	7.2	6	5	4

Product	1	2	3
Symbol	c_1	c_2	c_3
Contribution	30	20	25

Fig. 5.2

The product requirements are

$$50 \le y_1 \le 100$$
(5.5.2)
$$100 \le y_2 \le 140$$
$$80 \le y_3 \le 120$$

and the factor availabilities are

$$\sum_{i=1}^{2} x'_{i11} \le 400$$

Labor $$\sum_{i=1}^{3} x'_{i12} \le 200$$

$$\sum_{i=1}^{3} x'_{i13} \le 600$$

$$\sum_{i=1}^{3} x'_{i21} \le 150$$

Material

(5.5.3) $$\sum_{i=1}^{3} x'_{i21} \le 500$$

$$\sum_{i=1}^{2} x'_{i31} \le 30$$

$$\sum_{i=1}^{2} x'_{i32} \le 60$$

Machine Hrs. $$\sum_{i=1}^{2} x'_{i33} \le 30$$

$$\sum_{i=1}^{2} x'_{i34} \le 50$$

Fig. 5.3. Example limited substitution problem — simplex tableau form

Column groups (left → right): **Product 1** — Labor ($-9,\ -8,\ -7.5$), Mtl. ($-20,\ -12$), Mach. Hr. ($-6,\ -6,\ -5,\ -4$); **Product 2** — Labor ($-3.6,\ -4,\ -5$), Mtl. ($-8,\ -9$), Mach. Hr. ($-4,\ -5,\ -5,\ -8$); **Product 3** — Labor ($-M,\ -20,\ -15$), Mtl. ($-4,\ -3$); **Output** — $y_1\,(30)$, $y_2\,(20)$, $y_3\,(25)$.

Factors · $c_{ijk}\rightarrow$	-9	-8	-7.5	-20	-12	-6	-6	-5	-4	-3.6	-4	-5	-8	-9	-4	-5	-5	-8	$-M$	-20	-15	-4	-3	y_1	y_2	y_3	Ineq.	P_0
Production Function	1			1		1																		-1			$=$	0
		1			1		1																	-1			$=$	0
			1					1	1															-1			$=$	0
										1			1		1										-1		$=$	0
											1			1		1									-1		$=$	0
												1				1		1							-1		$=$	0
																			1			1				-1	$=$	0
																				1	1		1			-1	$=$	0
Factor Availabilities	5	4	3																								$\leq$	400
				5	4																						$\leq$	200
						1/1.2	1	1/.8	1																		$\leq$	600
										2	2	2															$\leq$	150
													3	3													$\leq$	500
															1/1.8	1/1.2	1	2									$\leq$	30
																			1	10	6						$\leq$	60
																						1	1				$\leq$	30
																											$\leq$	50
Output Bounds																								1			$\leq$	100
																								1			$\leq$	140
																									1		$\leq$	120
																							-1				$\leq$	-50
																								-1			$\leq$	-100
																									-1		$\leq$	-80

Factor Group	Labor			Material		Machine Hours				Output	R_{ik}		
Factoral Type / Product	1	2	3	1	2	1	2	3	4	y_i	R_{i1}	R_{i2}	R_{i3}
1	[-9] 50 [5]	[-8] [4]	[-7.5] [3]	[-20] 30 [5]	[-12] 20 [4]	[-6] 36 [1/1.2]	[-6] 14 [1]	[-5] [1]	[-4] [1/.8]	[100] [30] / [50] [<u>50</u>]	-7.5	-12	-9.6
2	[-3.6] 75 [2]	[-4] 25 [2]	[-5] [2]	[-8] [2]	[-9] 100 [3]	[-4] [1/1.8]	[-5] 55.2 [1/1.2]	[-5] 30 [1]	[-8] 14.8 [2]	[140] [20] / [100] [<u>100</u>]	-3	-9	-8
3	[-M] [1]	[-20] 15 [10]	[-15] 65 [6]	[-4] [1]	[-3] 80 [1]	X	X	X	X	[120] [25] / [80] [<u>80</u>]	-15	-3	X
Slack			210		40				20.4	$B-230$	0	0	0
Capacity	400	200	600	150	500	30	60	30	50	B			
K_{jk}	-.3	-.5	0	-1.6	0	4.32	3.6	3	0	0			

Limited Substitution Model

Value = 580.6

Fig. 5.4. First tableau

Applying the linear transformation shown in (5.4.7) to the x'_{ijk}'s and adding the artificial variable x_{311} with a cost of $\$M$, the problem may be comprehended in the tableau of Figure 5.3.

5.6. Computation Scheme Format

For computation purposes the variables are arranged in the form which is called "dyadic,"[1] as shown in Figure 5.4. Typical cell detail is given in Figure 5.5.

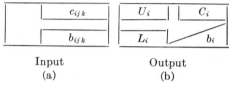

Input
(a)

Output
(b)

Fig. 5.5

The purpose of the b_i entry in Figure 5.5(b) is to allow an overall restriction on production

$$\text{(5.6.1)} \qquad \sum_{i=1}^{m} b_i y_i \leq B$$

to be placed on total production to take into account a total warehouse restriction, if desired. In the example, it is assumed that $b_i = 1$, for all i. B is a bound, sufficiently large so that it is greater than any possible Σy_i (i.e., the restrictions associated with B are "dummies" whose function is to preserve the rectangular form of the tableau).

5.7. Optimization Procedure

The computational details that have been devised may now be set forth as follows.

Initial Solution. The first step in finding an initial solution is to set $y_i = L_i$ for the products, underlining the entries to note that these bounded variables are equal to their lower bounds.[2] The dummy restriction is satisfied by entering $B = \Sigma y_i$ in the last column of the last row.

---

[1]Cf. Charnes, Cooper, and Miller (18).
[2]See (10) or (16).

The filling of the x_{ijk} entries follows the Northwest Corner Rule[1] of transportation type models, considering each of the factor groups as a subproblem in the transportation model, with the y_i column as the requirements column.[2] The machine-hour subproblem is considered as a reduced problem, satisfying only requirements 1 and 2, and hence having three rows (including slack) and four columns.

It will be noted from Figure 5.3 that there are seventeen equations (not including the bounding equations on y_i). The dummy restriction will add another, thus making the number of basis elements equal to eighteen. The filling-in process which has been used provides $m + n - 1$ entries[3] in each of the subproblems, as required for a basis, plus one $(B - \Sigma y_i)$. Thus the labor group provides $4 + 3 - 1 = 6$ elements; material provides $4 + 2 - 1 = 5$ elements; and machine hours, $3 + 4 - 1 = 6$ and $B - \Sigma_i$, 1 or a total of eighteen active basis elements. A glance at Figure 5.3 will reveal that, provided none of the y_i's are in the basis $(L_i < y_i < U_i)$, any two vectors which represent the coefficients for factors of different groups must be linearly independent. The method used for filling the squares in the subproblems assures linear independence of the vectors within the factor group, and the number of cells utilized therefore guarantees that an active basis is achieved. The rules, then, for handling the bounded variables guarantee that the entire space in which the problem is exhibited will be spanned.

Computation of the border entries. Following the method of Dantzig,[4] as expanded and generalized by Charnes and Cooper (18), the R_{ik}'s and K_{jk}'s are determined as follows

Rule (i)   Set $R_{ik} + b_{ijk}K_{jk} = c_{ijk}$

for all filled cells.   Also

(5.7.1)   (ia)   Set $R_{ik} = K_{jk} = 0$

for any cell in which positive slack appears, since then the theorem of

---

[1]For discussion of the "Northwest Corner Rule" and basis requirements for the transportation model, see (13).

[2]This process will cause no difficulty unless slack is a bounded variable. Should the case occur in which a slack variable must exceed its upper bound in order for $y_i = L_i$, the slack should be treated as an artificial vector with a lower bound equal to its original upper bound. As soon as the slack is reduced to its original upper bound, the slack variable can take on its original limits.

[3]*Ibid.*

[4](45a).

the alternative applies so that (when an optimum is attained) there will be the dual variables which are wanted.

With these conditions satisfied the test for optimality may be divided into two parts:

Rule (ii) $$R_{ik} + b_{ijk}K_{jk} \geq c_{ijk}$$

for all unoccupied factor squares. When all of these conditions are satisfied, no further substitution within a factor group can be profitable. This is a necessary condition for optimality, as may be proved mathematically; or following an easier course, it may be justified by economic consideration. A further necessary condition is

Rule (iia)
$$-\sum_k R_{ik} > c_i \qquad \text{for all } y_i = L_i$$

$$-\sum R_{ik} < c_i \qquad \text{for all } y_i = U_i$$

which will indicate that no further changes in production will be profitable.[1] These rules considered collectively are then seen to be both a necessary and sufficient condition for an optimum.[2]

Iteration procedure. Although it is not clear whether first proceeding with the substitution within groups will lead to an optimum in fewer iterations than first adjusting the production requirements, an apparent advantage of beginning with intra-group substitution is that, as long as $y_i = L_i$, the factor groups may be treated as separate transportation models in which iteration is relatively simple.[3]

The suboptimization within the factor groups proceeds exactly in the same fashion as that of the standard transportation model, hence will not be discussed.[4]

Figure 5.6 shows the tableau after the suboptimization has been performed, and the restrictions of Rule (ii) have been satisfied. Applying Rule (iia) to the revised tableau, it is noted that additional profit may be made by increasing the production of any of the three products.

Let y_1 be brought into the basis. The computational rule to effect the

---

[1]Since the dummy restriction was stated such that slack will always exist, it follows from the theorem of the alternative, that the corresponding dual variable will always be 0, and hence need not be considered.

[2]A proof, if desired, may be secured by reference to the Gale-Kuhn-Tucker dual theorem (45b).

[3]In fact, if production is stipulated exactly — i.e., $L_i = y_i = U_i$, the problem is trivial — and involves nothing more than the separate optimization of the subproblems.

[4]*Vide* (10), (13), and (45a).

Factor Group	Labor 1	Labor 2	Labor 3	Material 1	Material 2	Machine Hrs 1	Machine Hrs 2	Machine Hrs 3	Machine Hrs 4	Output y_i	R_{i1}	R_{i2}	R_{i3}
Product 1	-9 / 5	-8 / 4 (+10)	-7.5 / 3 (40)	-20 / 5	-12 / 4 (+50)	-6 / $\tfrac{1}{1.2}$	-6 / 1	-5 / 1 (+10)	-5 / $\tfrac{1}{.8}$	$\tfrac{30}{100}$	-8	-12	-5
Product 2		-4 / 2 (+10)	-5 / 2	-8 / 2	-9 / 3 (25)	$\tfrac{1}{1.2}$	-5 / $\tfrac{1}{1.2}$ (+26)	-5 / 1 (20)	-8 / 2	$\tfrac{50}{50}$	-3.6	-9	-5
Product 3	-3.6 / 2 (100), -M / 1	-20 / 10	-15 / 6 (80)	-4 / 1 (75)	-3 / 1 (80)	-4 / $\tfrac{1}{1.8}$ (54)			40	$\tfrac{20}{140}$	-16	-3	×
(cont.)										$\tfrac{100}{100}$	0	0	0
										$\tfrac{25}{120}$			
										$\tfrac{80}{80}$			
Slack	200	160	600	150	145	30	$38\tfrac{1}{3}$	30	50	B-230			
Capacity	400	200	600	150	500	30	60	30	50	B			
K_{jk}	0	0	$\tfrac{5}{3}$	.5	0	1.8	0	0	0	0			

Value $= \sum_i y_i \left(\sum_k R_{ik} + c_i \right) + \sum_{j,k} b_{jk} K_{jk} = 1199$

Fig. 5.6. Second tableau

Factor Group	Labor			Material		Machine Hours				Output	R_{ik}		
Factoral Type / Product	1	2	3	1	2	1	2	3	4	Y_i	R_{i1}	R_{i2}	R_{i3}
1	-9 5	-8 4 +30	-7.5 3 −40	-20 5 75	-12 4 70	-6 $\tfrac{1}{1.2}$ 54 $\tfrac{1}{1.8}$	-6 1 46 $\tfrac{1}{1.2}$	-5 1 30 1	-5 $\tfrac{1}{1.8}$ 40	30 / 100	-8	-12	-10
2	-3.6 2 100	-4 2	-5 2	-8 2	-9 3 25	-4 $\tfrac{1}{1.8}$	-5 $\tfrac{1}{1.2}$ $\overline{21\tfrac{2}{3}}$	-5 1	-8 2	70 / 50	-3.6	-9	-5
3	-M 1	-20 10	-15 6 +80	-4 1	-3 1 +80	✕	✕	✕	✕	20 / 140	-16	-3	✕
Slack	200	$\overline{80}$			$\overline{65}$					100 / 100 $\overline{B-250}$	0	0	0
Capacity	400	200	600	150	500	30	60	30	50	25 / 120 B			
K_{jk}	0	0	$\tfrac{5}{3}$	.5	0	1.8	0	5	4	80 / 80 0			

Value = 1299

Fig. 5.7. Third tableau

adjustments necessary for this are an adaptation of the stepping stone tours of Charnes and Cooper (13) which "surround" the cell into which y_i is to be brought with alternate $+$'s and $-$'s, utilizing the y_i column as an addend to the factor group tableau but reversing $+$ and $-$ signs in this column. In order to choose the vector to be eliminated it is necessary to choose the minimum of the ($-$) entries, adjusted by their coefficients. (If all $b_{ijk} = 1$ the least of the ($-$) entries numerically would be chosen.) In this case the limiting entry turns out to be x_{233}. The tableau is amended as shown in Figure 5.7 with y_1 no longer equal to its lower bound, and hence in the basis; whereas, while the ($+$) entries in the surrounding squares are *increased*, the ($-$) entries *decreased*. The border entries for the machine-hour group must be changed, with the restriction

$$(5.7.2) \qquad\qquad -\sum_k R_{1k} = c_1$$

substituted for the restriction

$$(5.7.3) \qquad\qquad R_{23} + b_{23}K_{32} = c_{233}.$$

Examination of the third tableau indicates that product 3 appears to have a much greater unit profit potential ($\$6.00$) than product 2 ($\$2.40$), so it will be brought into the basis. The product 3 square is surrounded as shown by the $+$'s and $-$'s in Figure 5.7. The limiting cell is slack labor type 2. The $+$'s are increased and the $-$'s decreased in both labor and materials. (Since no machine hours are required for product 3, these entries are unaffected, and since changing y_1 would require an additional basis vector in machine hours, paths including y_1 are not feasible.)

The fourth tableau reveals that x_{111} can profitably be brought into the basis. Place $+$ and $-$ signs in the paths which utilize alternating horizontal and vertical moves, including the y_i column, except that the signs are reversed in that column.[1] The minimum value is clearly $x_{113} = 20$. However, an increase in y_3 will take place. Should this

---

[1]The paths would appear to be

$$\overset{+}{x_{113}} \to \overset{-}{x_{313}} \to \overset{-}{y_3} \to \overset{+}{S} \to \overset{+}{S_{11}}$$

and

$$\overset{-}{y_1} \to \overset{+}{S} \to \overset{+}{S_{11}}$$

but the latter path would require an additional basis vector in machine hours similar to the situation in the third tableau. It will be noted that the introduction of one of the y_i's into one basis requires the removal from the basis of a vector in one of the factor subgroups. A reduction in that y_i would require an increase in one of the other y_i's thereafter — impossible in this instance since y_3 is not restricted by machine hours.

Factoral Type \ Product	Labor 1	Labor 2	Labor 3	Material 1	Material 2	Machine 1	Machine 2	Machine 3	Machine 4	Output y_i	R_{i1}	R_{i2}	R_{i3}
1	−9 / 5	−8 / 4	−7.5 / 3 (+20)	−20 / 5	−12 / 4 (70)	−6 / 1/1.2	−6 / 1	−5 / 1	−5 / 1/.8	30/100	−11	−12	−7
2	5 / 100 (+)	−4 / 2 (50)	−5 / 2	−8 / 2	−9 / 3 (25)	−4 / 1/.8	−5 / 1/1.2	−5 / 1	−8 / 2	70/50	−3.6	−9	−5
3	−3.6 / 2	−20 / 10	−15 / 6 (−90)	−4 / 1	−3 / 1 (90)	54	46	30	40	20/140	−22	−3	✕
Slack	−M / 1 (+200)			75	55		21 2/3			100/100, 25/120, 90/80, +B−260	0	0	0
Capacity	400	200	600	150	500	30	60	30	50	B			
K_{jk}	0	3/4	7/6	.5	0	1.8	0	2	1.6	0			

Value = 1359

Fig. 5.8. Fourth tableau

| Factor Group | Labor | | | Material | | Machine Hours | | | | Output | R_{ik} | | |
Factoral Type \ Product	1	2	3	1	2	1	2	3	4	Y_i	R_{i1}	R_{i2}	R_{i3}
1	−9 | 5 ; +20	−8 | 4 ; 50	−7.5 | 3	−20 | 5 ; 75	−12 | 4 ; 70	−6 | 1/1.2	−6 | 1 ; +46	−5 | 1 ; 30	−5 | 1/.8 ; 40	30 | 100	−9	−12	−9
2	−3.6 | 2 ; +100	−4 | 2	−5 | 2	−8 | 2	−9 | 3 ; +25	−4 | 1/1.8 ; 54	−5 | 1/1.2	−5 | 1	−8 | 2	70 | 50 · 20 | 140	−3.6	−9	−5
3	−M | 1	−20 | 10	−15 | 6 ; 100	−4 | 1	−3 | 1 ; 100	✕	✕	✕	✕	100 | 100 · 25 | 120 · 100 | 80	−22	−3	✕
Slack	− 100				− 45		$-21\frac{2}{3}$			$B-270$	0	0	0
Capacity	400	200	600	150	500	30	60	30	50	B			
K_{jk}	0	$\frac{1}{4}$	$\frac{7}{6}$	.5	0	1.8	0	4	3.2	0			

Value = 1399

Fig. 5.9. Fifth tableau

Factoral Type → / Product ↓	Labor 1	Labor 2	Labor 3	Material 1	Material 2	MH 1	MH 2	MH 3	MH 4	Output Y_i	R_{i1}	R_{i2}	R_{i3}
1	−9 ⟨5⟩ 20	−8 ⟨4⟩ 50	−7.5 ⟨3⟩	−20 ⟨5⟩ 75	−12 ⟨4⟩ 70	−6 ⟨1/1.2⟩ 54	−6 ⟨1⟩ 61	−5 ⟨1⟩	−5 ⟨1/.8⟩	100 | 30 ; 50 | 70	−9	−15.2	−5.8
2	−3.6 ⟨2⟩ 115	−4 ⟨2⟩	−5 ⟨2⟩	−8 ⟨2⟩	−9 ⟨3⟩ 40	−4 ⟨1/1.8⟩	−5 ⟨1/1.2⟩	−5 ⟨1⟩ 30	−8 ⟨2⟩ 40	140 | 20 ; 100 | 115	−3.6	−11.4	−5
3	−M ⟨1⟩	−20 ⟨10⟩ 10	−15 ⟨6⟩ 100	−4 ⟨1⟩ 100	−3 ⟨1⟩ 100	⊠	⊠	⊠	⊠	120 | 25 ; 80 | 100	−21.2	−3.8	⊠
Slack	70		100			30	$9\frac{1}{6}$			$B-285$	0	0	0
Capacity	400	200	600	150	500	30	60	30	50	B			
K_{jk}	0	$\frac{1}{4}$	$3\frac{1}{3}$	1.7	.8	1.8	0	.8	.64	0			

Value = 1435

Fig. 5.10. Sixth tableau — optimal

increase have caused another variable — say slack in material 2 — to become negative, then this variable should have been removed from the basis instead and the other entries adjusted accordingly. The fifth tableau is shown in Figure 5.9.

Profit can still be gained by introducing additional product 2. This is done, eliminating slack in material 2, and the obtained optimum tableau is shown in Figure 5.10.

The value of the program at each stage may be computed either from

$$(5.7.4) \qquad z = \sum_i c_i y_i - \sum_i \sum_j \sum_k c_{ijk} x_{ijk}$$

or, if desired, by[1]

$$z = \sum_i (c_i + \sum_k R_{ik}) y_i + \sum_j \sum_k b_{jk} K_{jk}$$

The gain at each stage of the tableau may be computed in simplex fashion. If the increase of the variable above 0 or its lower bound (or decrease from its upper bound) is denoted by Δx_{ijk} or Δy_i, as applicable, the increase is

$$(5.7.5) \qquad \Delta z = -\Delta x_{ijk}(R_{ik} + b_{ijk} K_{jk} - c_{ijk})$$

or

$$\Delta z = \Delta y_i(c_i + \Sigma R_{ik})$$

5.8. Power of the Model

Examination of the sixth tableau reveals that the criterion presented to the department head by his supervisor — profit maximization subject to output limitations — can be translated into operational instructions to the managers of the factor subgroups. For example, the labor manager can be instructed to:

1. Utilize all of labor type 3 in the manufacture of product 3.
2. Utilize all of labor type 2 in the manufacture of product 1.

---

[1]The first term of the summation will be 0 for $L_i < y_i < U_i$. The functional of the dual is

$$\sum_{j,k} b_{jk} K_{jk} + \tau_i U_i - \beta_i L_i$$

When $y_i = U_i$, the dual restriction must be satisfied exactly, or

$$c_i = -\sum_k R_{ik} + \tau_i$$

Similarly, when $y_i = L_i$

$$c_i = -\sum_k R_{ik} - \beta_i$$

3. Utilize labor type 1 on product 1 up to the point where the combined efforts of labor types 1 and 2 reach 70 units of product 1; utilize part of the remaining type 1 labor to produce 115 units of product 2; send the remaining type 1 labor home (or to the company labor pool).

Alternatively stated, the problem can now be handled by sub-optimization within the factor groups, taking the output stipulations found in the larger problem as the requirements. The *control* problem is now merely one of enforcing adherence to the production coefficients; i.e., the 600 hours of labor type 3 available must produce 100 units of product 3, etc. The intra-group relative seriousness of inefficiency in the various labor types can be comprehended in the dyadic format model tableau of Figure 5.11. It will be noted that, taking product require-

Product \ Labor Type	1	2	3	Required	R_i
1	20 [−9 / 5]	50 [−8 / 4]	0 [−7.5 / 3]	70	−9
2	115 [−3.6 / 2]	[−4 / 2]	[−5 / 2]	115	−3.6
3	[−M / 1]	[−20 / 10]	100 [−15 / 6]	100	−18
Slack	70				0
Capacity	400	200	600		
K_j	0	$\frac{1}{4}$	.5		

Labor Sub-optimization

Fig. 5.11. Transportation model

ments as given, the waste of 1 hour of type 3 labor costs $3.00. It is essentially the cost of an additional unit of product 3 ($18.00) divided by the number of hours required per unit of product (6). Alternatively, it is the cost of introducing a unit of slack at the hourly pay rate of $2.50, with the resulting $R_i + K_j - c_{ij} = \$3.00$. A similar waste of type 2 labor would result in an additional cost of $2.25 while a waste of type 1 labor would result only in a loss of $1.80, the hourly cost of the labor. Conversely, an improvement in the coefficients will produce cost savings of an equivalent amount. Therefore, the department head should set higher goals for the labor manager for efficiency of type 3 labor, relative to expected performance, than for type 2 and higher for type 2 than for type 1 (avoiding the error of setting the goals so high that they lose reality for the labor manager). Another possibility is to leave the intra-group optimization to the labor manager entirely, in which case the latter would set the goals for the various types of labor within his jurisdiction as indicated.

The model also provides the department head with information concerning capacity evaluations. Clearly each capacity whose K_{jk} has a positive value is a strategic factor. Is it possible that the 600 available hours of type 3 labor is an item which is established by "tradition?" Would it be possible to acquire this labor at a premium not to exceed $1.33 per hour? The model directs the department head's attention to the possibility of obtaining one type of additional labor or another, as opposed to the more nebulous form in which this question is often asked; i.e., "Should we or should we not hire more workers?" Furthermore, he can compute the gain from hiring additional labor. Hiring 120 more hours of labor type 3 would enable him to increase his production of product 3 to the upper limit of 120 units with a resulting increase in profit of $160 less any premium he would need to pay above the standard rate of $2.50 per hour.

An interesting contrast between this model and "management by exception" develops in the context of paying a premium for a factor in order to increase profit. From the mathematical properties of the optimal solution to the linear programming problem, the increase in the amount of any factor for which $K_{jk} > 0$ will result in increased profit, even if a premium (less than K_{jk}) must be paid on the additional units. Assume that the c_{ij}'s are both standard and actual unit cost. A supervisor who chose to pay the premium to increase the "profit" of his department would, under a standard cost system, incur an unfavorable cost variance. Hence, under a usual scheme of "management by exception," he would at least be required to file a report to show cause but would not receive compensatory reward. In other words he would not be motivated to increase profit at the sacrifice of one of his "black" variances. Thus the paramaterization has pointed up an apparent flaw in the principle of "management by exception." In its concentration on unfavorable variances, it creates a situation in which it is not desirable to increase one cost by some amount in order to increase profit by a larger amount.

The complete absence of slack in the material subgroup has additional implications. First of all, the absence of slack in any factor group which contains required inputs for all the outputs (or a set of subgroups without slack which, among them, contain inputs for all of the outputs) renders the set of optimum outputs a Pareto point. Hence, the material subgroup in the example and, generally speaking, any slackless factor group taken as a whole is a strategic factor. If, in response to his supervisor's orders, the department head is required to increase the output of one of the products, he must choose either decreasing the output of one of the others or finding some way of altering the restrictions of the slackless group(s).

5.9. Parametric Programming of the Model[1]

Changing the contributions of the outputs does not indicate, at least in the example, great sensitivity of the production schedule to these "intra-company trading prices." Although the optimum shown is valid only for \$29.20 $\leq c_1 \leq$ \$30.20, y_1 is increased to $81\frac{1}{4}$, y_2 decreased to its lower limit of 100 for \$30.20 $\leq c_1 \leq$ \$43.00. Between \$43.00 and \$50.00, y_1 increases another $4\frac{13}{28}$ units with a $17\frac{6}{7}$ unit decrease in y_3, while a $c_1 \geq$ \$50.00 is needed to drive y_3 to its lower limit. No change in strategic factors is noted until the contribution exceeds \$50.00, when labor type 2 is added to the group. Machine hours type 2 are added to the basis replacing y_2, labor type 3 replaces labor type 1 allocated to product 1, and slack in labor type 2 replaces y_3 at the points of discontinuity indicated above. Information of this kind is, of course, invaluable to the supervisor in determining the effect of "errors" in the trading prices on production schedules.

Treating the capacities of the strategic factors as parameters where their expansion is a possibility will also yield valuable information. For

---

[1]For parameterizations via efficient (Pareto) points see the method described by Charnes and Cooper in "Theory and Computation for Delegation Models; *K*-Efficiency, Functional Efficiency and Goals" (14).

example, it is advantageous to increase the availability of material 2 to 533 units, provided the premium is not more than $0.80 per unit; an increase of still another 7.35 units is justified provided the premium is not more than $0.30 per unit; no increase above 540.35 units is profitable unless one of the capacities of the other strategic factors is changed. Perhaps the most valuable aspect of the parametric programming is the preparation of a schedule of priorities so that the department head can, as his time permits, investigate, or cause to be investigated, the extension of those restrictions which seem to produce the most severe limitations on his activity.

5.10. Extension of the Model to the Next Higher Level in the Hierarchy

The outputs of the department, y_i, constitute a set of factors seen by the supervisor of several departments. Together with the outputs of other departments, they form the raw materials for the outputs of the multi-department unit. Although it may seem at first circular to call the contributions of the original problem the costs for the multi-department unit, the ability of the supervisor to investigate the possibility of obtaining additional input by paying a premium (i.e., raising the contribution per unit output in the original problem) provides a framework for intercommunication between the levels without the supervisor actually investigating the behavior of the factors in the original problem. Furthermore he can, for short-run problems, forcibly raise the requirements of certain outputs of the departments, obtaining from them the cost of so doing (from the R_{ik}'s of the original problem).

It is quite conceivable that a compounding of such models could be developed so that the outputs at each level could serve as the inputs to the next, etc., in such a way that an optimum optimorum could be found. This development, however, is beyond the scope of this thesis. Nevertheless, the work of Charnes, Cooper, and Miller (18) toward developing an algorithm for the construction of algorithms strongly suggests that it may be possible to devise models at each level which would be appropriate to the organization at each level. Pending the development of such an algorithm, the hierarchical formulation[1] rests on existing models which, in the main (the model of this thesis excepted) were not developed for the primary purpose of coordinating the activities of groups.

---

[1]Not to be confused with the "hierarchical model" of linear programming — *vide* Cooper and Charnes (10), or of experimental design — *vide* Kempthorne(41).

5.11. Summary

It should be emphasized once again that the above model was devised for studying the problems of planning and coordination. In particular, it has been an attempt at devising a scheme for coordinating control efforts in a multi-department situation. Developed specifically for the purpose of studying the interrelationships of factors in logical grouping rather than individually, it lends itself naturally to the study of more or less separated collections of activities in a firm. Through its relatively simple computation techniques, it is possible to assess the effect on output of variations in the input of any of the factors in any of the groups. Furthermore, it is possible to study the effect of the availability of a factor in one of the groups on the usage in another.

Thus the model provides a vehicle for the study of substitutability and complementarity of factors in a setting which more closely resembles the operation of an actual firm than the classical economic model of the firm. The increase in availability of one of the factors may lead to an increased usage of another in one of the other groups of factors — i.e., "factor cooperancy" — but may cause no change in some of the others. Or, an increase in availability in one of the factors in a subgroup may exhibit "factor rivalry," causing a decrease in use of another, although (at least within certain limits) it may not. In either case the model offers a convenient means of studying these relationships.

Returning to issues which are more closely related to this thesis, its relevance to specific types of planning should be noted. From the standpoint of planning for capital expenditures, the model (provided the costs and contributions are accurate) is an extremely convenient device for determining total cost or profit under various equipment plans, e.g., machine hour capacities. Similarly, planned expansion or contraction in various segments of the labor force may be tested with the aid of the model.[1]

Utilizing an essentially Marshallian (60) concept, the effect of prices on output can be studied under assumptions which do not require infinite substitutability of all production factors. Furthermore, the effect of changes in output "prices" on the prices which could (or should) be paid to increase the availability of factors can be studied through the dual variables of the linear programming formulation. Having implications both with regard to planning and control, the effectiveness of using

---

[1]This process of varying the capacity restrictions — i.e., parametric programming in the dual — is essentially equivalent to the systematic varying of costs or contributions in the direct problem.

intra-company trading prices as a control device (with rate of profit increase or a profit goal as a criterion of efficiency) can be studied along with the necessary coordination of inputs of one "control unit" with the outputs of another under such a scheme.

Some further inference may be drawn with respect to control viewed in the light of one individual controlling several interdependent factors (or departments) rather than as the single factor control dealt with elsewhere in this paper. First of all, the dual variables give "clues" as to where it is important to attempt to carefully control certain factors. In the context presented by Charnes and Cooper (11), the model can be used to at least determine some priorities in the allocation of supervisors' time.

Also, the possibility of actually preventing an increase in profit through certain types of control is apparent by the use of the model. In particular, "management by exception" which deals primarily with unfavorable deviations from standard may produce a suboptimization in terms of the price or usage of one or more factors which does not lead to optimization in the large. A possible implication is that both positive and negative (favorable and unfavorable) variances must be examined in an effective control system.

The development of a hierarchy of such (or similar) models would be very desirable for the extension of the power of this one-department model to the multi-level organization met in practice. Pending such development, however, the implications of the model for coordination at any level may be used, with reservations, of course, implied by the dangers of local optima.

To carry this analysis somewhat further, it is to be noted that suboptimization within any subgroup will not produce an overall optimum *unless* the output stipulations of the overall optimum are restrictions on the subproblems. Furthermore, examination of the optimal tableau indicates that in some instances, the cheapest means of producing product equivalents is not always used. That is, a product equivalent of two factors may be produced most cheaply by the use of the same factor. However, the relative advantage of one may be far greater than for the other, and hence this former may well utilize all or most of this cheapest factor. If the cost of each product is separately controlled, it may lead to some compromise in order to prevent negative variances in one of the costs. The deleterious effect of such individual product control of costs within the subgroup would be accentuated if the standard for the product whose relative advantage was greater was "loose," the other "tight."

Thus the criteria of "accurate costs" and "control exercised on an individual product basis in every department where possible" applied to standards are shown, through use of the model, to produce nonoptimal results. In the case described, the standard for the product whose relative advantage for the use of the shared factor is greater should be "tight" and the other "loose," *ceteris paribus*, to produce an optimal result. Furthermore, the criteria for the setting of individual standards are not independent of the output requirements and hence are not independent of the activities (and standards) of the other subgroups. No amount of time and effort spent on the setting of "accurate" engineering standards for an individual activity can eliminate this interdependence.

The model thus points out the need for a thorough re-evaluation of the criteria of setting of budgets and standards. It suggests the study of the planned use of incorrect information in setting individual standards which would lead to an optimum in the large.

CHAPTER 6

Summary and Directions for Further Research

6.1. Introduction

The preceding chapter concludes the substantive and methodological presentations for this thesis. This chapter will attempt to (1) draw together in summary fashion some of the main points and conclusions, (2) establish some degree of relevance to the existing literature in budgetary (and related) practice, and (3) indicate possible directions which appear promising for further research. In passing through this order of topics it will also be possible to point up (still further) certain shortcomings and gaps in the present study which are pertinent to possible attempts at actual application.

The main body of the thesis may be divided as follows:

1. An introductory statement of the problem of budgetary control, its setting, and the motivation underlying this study (Chapter 1).
2. An analytical model to establish certain broad qualitative features of the topic to be studied in more precise form (Chapter 2).
3. A survey (and assessment) of relevant bodies of scientific hypotheses and supporting experimental evidence and, to a lesser extent, managerial experience which could be used to point up issues both of theory and date inadequacy (Chapter 3).
4. A report of an experiment undertaken to test certain major parts of the theory presented as well as collateral issues which are relevant to psychology, economics, and management practice (Chapter 4).

5. Finally, a new analytical model along with a method of solution and analysis designed to (a) highlight certain features, such as interdepartmental effects considered over a hierarchy, which were not specifically covered in the preceding materials and to (b) state preliminary propositions which appear plausible enough to warrant further investigation; to do so, moreover, in a way which is not so ambiguous as to escape any possibility of scientific verification or rejection by recourse to suitably controlled situations.[1]

6.2. Planning and Control

At this stage of the analysis it is well to note certain differences between the approach used in Chapter 5 and elsewhere in this thesis. Whereas most of the emphasis has been on controls applied to individual behavior, the model of Chapter 5 is oriented as well towards interactions and coordination of a purely planning nature.[2] The latter is thus more closely akin to the kind of approach (alternative costs considered *mutatis mutandis*) which has been typical in economic analysis and which has been carried over into operations research. It is based on a consideration of alternatives *as if* the alternative chosen will in fact be carried out to a reasonable degree of approximation. This theory is best viewed in terms of an individual decision-making model where (assuming adequate physiological responses) the organism may be expected to react faithfully and exactly to its own commands. In such a system[3] there is no real problem of goal discrepancies (e.g., of a budget vs. aspiration level variety), and virtually everything reduces to the question of whether accuracy and felicity are present in the costs and benefits that have been

---

[1]It is believed that the model and methods adduced in Chapter 5 make some contribution to the planning literature (and methodology) as found in management science, operations research, etc. — especially to that part of the literature (and research) which is concerned with "model types." On the other hand, this is not the main objective here since, unlike the typical applications in management science, the purpose is ultimately to devise certain explicit tests that involve motivation and control elements. Thus, for this purpose, it is hoped ultimately to devise a suitable experiment which would test the consequences of supplying programming results of an optimizing variety to subordinates, as against other kinds of information, in order to ascertain when, and under what circumstances, one or the other of these kinds of information might be preferable.

[2]Cf. Charnes and Cooper, (10) for a further discussion of the difference between "planning" and "control," and Chapter 1 of this thesis.

[3]At least with the assumptions which are usually used in the analyses.

calculated.[1] It follows that there also is no problem which can result from the effects of goal discrepancies upon performance.

In contrast to this "economic-planning" approach — which at first seems to be of a multi-person variety but is, in reality, a single-person multiple-factor approach — even the single-person model of this paper is seen to be a multiple-person approach. (Otherwise goal discrepancies could not be maintained.) The issue of "rational" calculation is then seen to assume dimensions which are different from those which might be expected to apply to planning considerations only, i.e., interpersonal dimensions. For control (as distinct from planning) purposes the utilization of accurate calculations and the transmission of their results to others may be beneficial, neutral, or harmful depending on (a) the kinds of persons and tasks involved, (b) the setting in which operations are conducted, and (c) the vehicle and the time sequences, etc., utilized for information transmittal.

A servomechanical analogy may be helpful.[2] As is well known, the accuracy of calibrations and the speed of response to changes in the system (or the environment) that may, or should, be incorporated in such a mechanism cannot be decided apart from other characteristics of the system. It is possible, for example, that more "accurate" or more timely — or even more timely and accurate — "feedback" of information may fail to improve performance and may even have harmful effects. While it is not proposed to push this analogy with servomechanisms to absurd limits, it seemed plausible to suppose that systems involving humans, or humans and machines, might be subject to the same general kinds of considerations. Thus, an hypothesis which is part of certain servomechanism designs, deals with issues involving rates of change (rather than levels) imposed on certain control elements and the effects that such changes may have on performance. The experimental evidence is wholly compatible with this hypothesis and stands in rather sharp contrast to much of the literature of budgeting (and economics), which is preoccupied with "levels" and the accuracy thereof.

It should be said, however, that most of the situations envisioned in

---

[1]In fact, a good deal of the literature in economics is concerned with formulating methods — graphs, calculus, linear programming, etc. — to facilitate such calculations and/or prescribing certain necessary or sufficient conditions which may be used to verify whether the wanted results will be achieved.

[2]If a justification for this analogy is desired, it may be secured from the comments of W. W. Cooper and H. A. Simon. See their commentary on the paper by F. Modigliani and H. Sauerlender in *Short Term Economic Forecasting* (42a,b), pp. 352 ff.

the industrial literature do not have learning components involving the same orders of magnitude for rates of learning that were present in the experiment.[1] On the other hand, there is no reason to assume that all operations are conducted along the frontier provided by an optimal production function, as is assumed in economics. Nor is there reason to assume that the general prescription of budgets ("not-too-loose, but attainable") which is virtually ubiquitous in the management literature is always "best" — or even generally "best."[2]

While rules for change are given in the management literature on budgeting, these are generally assumed to be required only when structural changes (e.g., due to technological alterations) occur, *provided* the budget level was "accurate" in the first place. In particular, the idea of using change (at suitable rates and upwards as well as downwards) as a control instrument per se is not systematically discussed and, for the most part, is not even mentioned.[3] Both the experiment and the analytical model which preceded it indicate circumstances in which "levels," however "accurate," will not induce performance which is both possible and desirable. On the other hand, when rates of change are to be used then more careful analyses (and more powerful techniques) are required since, under certain circumstances, their use may have explosive effects with highly deleterious consequences.[4]

However the particular details of the experiment and model may be viewed, it seems at least reasonable to suppose that it is a proper task of budgetary control to be concerned with strategies for constant improvement of performance. This cannot be done, of course, and it even reduces to nonsense if the presuppositions of economic theory are adopted. No explicit test has been made of the hypothesis that

---

[1] But see footnote 1, p. 67, *supra*. Although the rates of learning might not be comparable, according to the definition of task difficulty defined by Chapman, Kennedy, Newell, and Biel (8), the rate of change of difficulty of the experimental task could be approximated in the industrial task.

[2] As has been repeatedly noted, the literature of budgeting (and industrial engineering) and the literature of economics are not wholly consistent, relative to each other, in their assumptions or even in their use of the term "best."

[3] This may possibly be the result of reactions to the hostile criticisms of labor (and others) to early industrial engineering practice, which is supposed to have utilized directed incentives for unilateral and unidirectional changes in worker performance requirements. It seems equally plausible to believe, however, that is is rather a byproduct of the emphasis on "accuracy."

[4] This is well documented in the servomechanical literature and is explicitly considered (in a somewhat different fashion) in postulate (iiic) of the analytical model discussed in Chapter 2.

individual firms do, in fact, operate on an optimum production function although, as pointed out in Chapter 1, the studies of Cyert, Dill, and March (23) and Lanzillotti (47) offer evidence to the contrary. For whatever it is worth — and it is not offered as valid scientific evidence — the reference to standards that are "not-too-loose, but attainable," which appears in many parts of the management literature, may be offered as an example that the assumed situation does not obtain ubiquitously. It is difficult, moreover, to believe that most plants are actually so well run and so well organized that a supervisor cannot effect some further improvements even though the state of technology is already well fixed. In addition, it is not always clear just what is meant by the technological optimum. Consider, for instance, a student who fails to make a perfect score on an examination. The technical knowledge being available (at least to the instructor), does this mean that the student fails to achieve an optimum even though his performance was brilliant? Or, to address both the management and economics literature, does a fundamental (technological) change take place whenever a virtuoso renders a new and better interpretation of a known piece of music? A chess or bridge player may, through practice, learn to improve his game even though no fundamental change in rules is involved. To come closer to the problems of the individual firm, it has been observed that typists and secretaries improve their performance over repeated trials with their machines and/or their bosses.

It is not proposed to be unduly critical in these observations or even to overdraw the distinctions between planning and control. In practical situations the two (e.g., the budget as a plan and as a control) may well be confounded and, as already noted,[1] even the planning model discussed in Chapter 5 may be extended for control studies. Consider, for example, the light it might throw on the calculation (and use) of "accurate" (levels) of standards and the "principle of exceptions." One version of the principle of exceptions involves symmetric reporting of both favorable and unfavorable "variances."[2] Another involves reporting (and presumably investigation) of unfavorable variances only. The presumption in the first case is that knowledge of causes is desirable for future improvement as well as immediate correction. The second focuses on the latter only, perhaps depending on other devices such as

---

[1]Cf., *supra*, p. 3 ff. and p. 141.

[2]This term is used in its accounting rather than its statistical sense. See, however, R. M. Cyert and G. Meyers (80a) for an application of statistical principles as a guide to variance reporting, as well as a suggestion as to how these techniques may be used to determine relatively tight and loose standards.

informal observation or, possibly, periodic investigation to determine whether structural changes sufficient to warrant a change in standard have occurred. In either case it is generally presumed, perhaps according to some ordering, that an expenditure of managerial time and attention is warranted and that the effects will be beneficial — or at least not baneful.

This topic, conditions for reporting variances and (higher level) managerial invention, can (and it is hoped will) be investigated. But even before this is done the model of Chapter 5 demands that certain other issues related to accurate standards and variance reports (principle of exceptions) be attended to. In particular, the parameterization techniques revealed certain cases where a premium (above standard) was warranted. This means that if the variance were eliminated and the standard were reduced to the level where it faithfully reflected the true performance possibility of an individual department, then if the investigation were successful in bringing performance into line, an overall worsening would occur. Thus, at the cost of managerial time and effort, the profits of the entity would be reduced.

It does not follow, of course, that a report of the true dual values to the supervisor of this department would necessarily produce the desired result either. All that can be said at this juncture is that the topic is one which warrants serious investigation, and this is one among other issues which the model of Chapter 5 has helped to uncover — and in a form which may be readily extended for future testing.

6.3. Some Selected Quotations

At this point it may be well to introduce selected quotations from the management literature which will help to supply perspective on the preceding comments and to prepare the way for the concluding portion of this chapter, which deals with some limitations of the present study and indicates some possible future directions for research. It has not been possible to draw upon a representative sample of this literature, so the author's choice and possible biases should be allowed for. On the other hand, an effort was made to be fair, and quotations were selected which would not merely document the previous comments but would also serve to indicate some of the qualifications that writers in the field typically employ in their presentations.[1]

---

[1]As a result some of the statements may appear unnecessarily vague. This seems, however, to be an unavoidable consequence of eliminating from inclusion in this series statements of a more clear and succinct character which, out of context, might appear merely as an attempt at setting up a series of "straw men."

Consider, first, the following statements from Rautenstrauch and Villers (64), which give their views on budgeting for fixed and variable expense:

> The *fixed expense* which does not vary with production is budgeted as for the previous period, unless some fundamental changes have been made involving fixed charges. If, for instance, some new equipment has been bought, the depreciation expense is increased. The budgeting of the fixed expense does not as a rule encounter any serious difficulty.
>
> The *variable expense* — The same can be said of the variable component of the factory overhead (such as indirect material). Past records will generally provide the necessary data. As the variable expense varies directly with production, the data will easily be recomputed in terms of the future rate of production, according to the production budget.[1]

These all-purpose statements are intended to cover in somewhat mechanical fashion all sorts of "human" and "business" situations. The budget pattern of the experiment which best approximates the procedures outlined is the "low" budget. The logically derived result of a static budget in the mathematical model is a static cost. In the standard procedures described there is no incentive for the search for and alteration of strategic factors described in Chapter 5.

The following questions might now be asked: Is it necessarily true that "fundamental changes" *must* be made (even assuming an "accurate" budget) before scheduling an improvement in performance? What is said of the reverse problem of when (e.g., via search stimulation) a request for authorizing new equipment should take place at the departmental level? In addition, what incentive (and risks) should be provided for this purpose? Clearly there is a possible interaction between fixed and variable expense that may be possible in many conceivable situations. There is a further need for considering possible interdepartmental reactions of the kind discussed in Chapter 5, and this is far from being a *simple* problem (with past records providing the necessary data); it involves, as a matter of reporting and budgeting design, very subtle problems in economics and psychology. How, in general, is the possibility of continued improvement in performance to be handled — or is this problem irrelevant as an issue of budgeting?

The above quotations are from a standard text in industrial engineering.[2] One of the better books on budgeting presented from an

---

[1] (64), pp. 132-133.

[2] Cf. the short biographical note on Dr. Villers (and his association with the late Dr. Rautenstrauch) which appears opposite his article, "Industrial Budgeting," pp. 1073 ff., in W. G. Ireson and E. L. Grant (38).

accounting standpoint is J. Brooks Heckert's *Business Budgeting and Control* (34). It may be useful, therefore, to turn to this source for a quotation on another of the topics mentioned in this thesis. After making a clear (and cogent) distinction between standards (for judging performance) and budgets (for planning purposes),[1] Heckert goes on to say:

> In many concerns where operations have become highly standardized, the distinction (i.e., between budget and standard costs) tends to disappear and the budget figures serve, generally speaking, both as measures of performance and as a coordinating tool. This is particularly true in regard to production operations and costs and the more mechanical aspects of distribution activities; however, the distinction seldom disappears entirely.[2]

It is not clear whether Heckert regards this tendency to coalescence as good or bad. More perceptive than many authors, he also tends to be more careful and guarded in his presentations. Within the limits of a possible interpretation, however, the following questions might be raised. Insofar as the two sets of external goals on the same data (e.g., costs) fail to coalesce, how much of a discrepancy should be tolerated? Is there some degree of discrepancy which constitutes a (psychological or logical) contradiction either in a department or over the entire system? If a contradiction is caused, what are its consequences for performance?[3] If coalescence is to be encouraged, at what rate should it be introduced? More generally, what relations should such external goals bear (a) to internal goals, such as aspiration levels, and (b) to performance?

In contrast to the extremely mechanical emphasis of most of the budgetary literature, the following statement by Heckert on sales quotas (and their relations to standards) is of interest:

> Actual experience with sales quotas, as with all standards, will reveal that sales representatives react to them somewhat differently, particularly at first. Some are stimulated to their highest efficiency, while

---

[1]The distinction drawn by Heckert is related to, but not identical with, the one previously made in this chapter — i.e., the distinction between the budget as a plan and as a control instrument. Actually, the distinction used in this thesis is developed in an unpublished manuscript by W. W. Cooper (21), "Historical Cost and Alternative Cost," to which I was given access.

[2](34), p. 10.

[3]Cf. Charnes and Cooper, "Silhouette Functions of Cost Behavior" (12), *Quarterly Journal of Economics*, for a discussion of possible contradictions (in a logical sense) and also their discussion "On The Theory and Computation of Delegation Models" (14) for a discussion of the possible use of contradictions in managerial planning along with a specification of analytical methods for dealing with these problems in a mathematical context.

others are discouraged. Some sales executives place considerable emphasis upon this human element in setting their quotas. In general, however, good men will, in the long run, respond favorably to intelligently devised quotas, particularly when compensation is fairly adjusted to performance.[1]

Although the meaning of "intelligently devised quotas" is not amplified, the above remarks tend to imply that "some sales executives" probably have a better plan for improving performance through budgeting than those described in the traditional books on budgeting. Certain fairly obvious questions may be raised about parts of the statements as quoted, but it is perhaps best to let the matter rest here in order to turn attention to some other topics which are at least indirectly relevant to what Heckert seems to prescribe.

Apt statements may be found almost at will on the principle of exceptions. It is therefore of interest to indicate that, under the conditions over which it was conducted, the experiment indicates that variations from standard are neither an accurate measure of performance nor an accurate guide to improvement in performance. Thus budget attainment in the "low" budget[2] groups was relatively high but performance was relatively low. According to these experimental results, the difficulty of achievement must either be arrived at by the frequency of attainment (i.e., a statistical analysis of past data) or by some independent measure (e.g., a problem-solving equivalent of Methods Time Measurement). This type of measurement would be referred to in practice as an "engineering standard," and to this extent the findings may tend to justify some of the distinctions and emphases found in the literature.

On the other hand, the experiment offers some evidence for limitations on the value of "engineering standards." At the beginning of the experiment the performance capabilities on this task were almost unknown to the experimenter. Had 10,800 subjects been tested under a situation in which, for example, no rewards were present, the increment in information applicable to the choice between a high and a low budget would have been insignificant. The results indicate that performance in a problem-solving task is really not determinate except under conditions in which the goals and rewards are specified.

To draw some summary conclusions on this literature the following observations are offered. Two important features seem to be lacking if

---

[1] (34), p. 138.

[2] Recall that this is the one which corresponds to the case usually recommended, "not-too-loose, but attainable."

budgetary practice is to be judged by this literature. The first is a lack of a systematic empirical approach or of any systematic research that can serve as a basis for generalizations, evaluation, and further progress. If standards are to be set on the basis of historical cost and/or engineering standards, the possibility of attaining better performance by the simple means of expecting it (or at least convincing the department head that better performance is expected) is a phenomenon which, if investigated, is not reported in the extant literature.

The maintenance of a static budget and its possible failure to induce improvement in performance when that is possible has already been commented upon. The effects of rate changes and the conditions or amounts in which they might be applied are, by and large, ignored. To turn the usual point of view around, one wonders what would happen if the budget department were scored by red and black variances by reference to a technological optimum or ideal standard (if one could be constructed) of possible budgetary practice.

The second of the two observations to be made is the curious phenomenon of a tendency toward persistent disregard for the motivation structure, even at the level of the individual manager, despite the preoccupation of many other parts of managerial literature with this kind of problem. Emphasis is on "accuracy" of the budget, not its relationship to the desires, capabilities, or varying situations in which a person who is held to such a budget may possess when he receives it. Exceptions may be cited (as in the above quotation drawn from Heckert). Having said this much, however, it should probably also be said that many of the written rules are tempered in practice; some may be wholly replaced and rules and procedures may also be employed that are not reported in the standard literature. This in itself, however, would be unfortunate and might be counted as a "lack." Perhaps a greater and more extended use of analytical models might have further use than as a guide to laboratory experiments, qualitative characterizations, or statistical-mathematical analyses. The explicit and exact statement that such models require might serve as a standard of reference against which new procedures or significant deviations in old procedures might be detected and judged. If this could be accompanied by publication then a foundation for rapid progress in business practice and scientific understanding in this important area of management might be secured.[1]

---

[1]The reference is to "control." Numerous mathematical models and modes of analyses for various phases of "planning" — e.g., for ascertaining or imputing the cost of funds — are, of course, already available.

6.4. Some Directions for Further Research

It has probably not escaped the reader's attention that I have perhaps been more harsh than can be justified in my statements about the budgeting literature. If this is true then some amelioration is due these authors. It can perhaps be attained by emphasizing, at the close of this thesis, certain highly important topics which have not been covered in either the analytical models or experimental results. This will be done in a form which suggests some further avenues of research.

1. No attempt was made to analyze either timeliness or content of budget or accounting reports. Is understandability (hence simplicity or directness) a desideratum, as is often assumed? If so, are uniform reports to all individuals a proper medium for attaining this goal? Is there a dynamics (e.g., of learning) which should be allowed for?

2. Only a short span of time was covered in the experiments. Would the effects uncovered hold true over longer spans, or would some of them weaken and others arise to take their place? In terms of the possible correctives suggested (or implied) at various points in the presentation of this thesis, the following quotation from P. A. Samuelson is particularly apt: "[I] . . . wish to point out the possible occurrence in economic systems of the common medical phenomena whereby short term remedies may have long term deleterious effects."[1] This kind of possibility was not even considered in its own right in the analytical models presented.

3. The question of intervention rules for superiors in the hierarchical model was not explored, so this thesis, like some of the writers quoted, is subject to criticism on this score.

4. The relation of the internal environment of the individual to that of the firm and the relation of the latter (or, better, both) to the broader setting of society was not examined. What effects may be expected from this quarter on (a) aspiration level and (b) performance by both superiors and subordinates?

Many other questions and deficiencies might be noted but enough, by now, has probably been said. To close, it is well to emphasize once more that this thesis has been submitted only as part of a scientific inquiry in an important area of management. If it arouses some interest even in criticizing, repairing, or extending some of the deficiencies of this study, it will have served its purpose.

---

[1](69), p. 355 (In 1947 ed.). In spite of the obvious veracity of this statement and its often unrecognized applicability, it has apparently been omitted from the later edition.

BIBLIOGRAPHY*

(1) Anthony, R. N., "Cost Concepts for Control," *The Accounting Review,* Vol. 32, No. 2, April, 1957.

(2) Argyris, C., *The Impact of Budgets on People,* Ithaca, New York: Prepared for The Controllership Foundation, Inc., at Cornell University, 1952.

(3) Barnard, C. I., *The Function of the Executive,* Cambridge: Harvard University Press, 1954.

(4) Birch, H. G., "The Role of Motivational Factors in Insightful Problem Solving," *Journal of Comparative Psychology,* Vol. 38, 1945, pp. 295–317.

(5) Carlson, S., *A Study on the Pure Theory of Production,* New York: Kelly and Millman, Inc., 1956.

(6) Chance, June E., "Generalization of Expectancies as a Function of Need Relatedness," Unpublished Doctor's Dissertation, The Ohio State University, 1952, cited in J. B. Rotter (67).

(7) Chapman, D. W., and J. Volkmann, "A Social Determinant of the Level of Aspiration," *Journal of Abnormal Psychology,* Vol. 34, 1939, pp. 225–238.

(8) Chapman, R. L., J. L. Kennedy, A. Newell, and W. C. Biel, "The Systems Research Laboratory's Air Defense Experiments," *Management Science,* Vol. 5, No. 3, April, 1959.

(9) Charnes, A., "Optimality and Degeneracy in Linear Programming," *Econometrica,* Vol. 20, No. 2, April, 1952.

(10) Charnes, A., and W. W. Cooper, "Management Models and Industrial Applications of Linear Programming," *Management Science,* 4, No. 1, October, 1957.

(11) Charnes, A., and W. W. Cooper, "Optimization in New Item Production," Third Annual George Washington University — ONR Logistic Conference, January, 1952.

(12) Charnes, A., and W. W. Cooper, "Silhouette Functions of Short Run Cost Behavior," *Quarterly Journal of Economics,* February, 1954.

---

*This listing does not claim to be a complete bibliography of budget control or even a complete listing of those works consulted during the preparation of the thesis. It contains only those works which were specifically referred to in the text and footnotes.

(13) Charnes, A., and W. W. Cooper, "The Stepping Stone Method of Explaining Linear Programming Calculations in Transportation Problems," *Management Science*, Vol. 1, No. 1, October, 1954.

(14) Charnes, A., and W. W. Cooper, "Theory and Computation for Delegation Models: K Efficiency, Functional Efficiency and Goals," Northwestern University ONR Project, *Temperal Planning and Management Decision Under Risk and Uncertainty;* and Pittsburgh: Carnegie Institute of Technology ONR Project, *Planning and Control of Industrial Operations*, December, 1958.

(15) Charnes, A., W. W. Cooper, and A. Henderson, *An Introduction to Linear Programming*, New York: John Wiley and Sons, Inc., 1952.

(16) Charnes, A., and C. E. Lemke, "Computational Theory of Linear Programming I: The Bounded Variables Problem," ONR Research Memorandum No. 10, (mimeo), Pittsburgh: Carnegie Institute of Technology, Graduate School of Industrial Administration, January, 1954.

(17) Charnes, A., W. W. Cooper, and B. Mellon, "A Model for Optimization Production by Reference to Cost Surrogates," *Econometrica*, Vol. 23, No. 3, July, 1955.

(18) Charnes, A., W. W. Cooper, and M. H. Miller, "Dyadic Problems and Sub-Dual Methods," (mimeo), Pittsburgh: Carnegie Institute of Technology, Graduate School of Industrial Administration, Office of Naval Research Project on Planning and Control of Operations Research; and Purdue University, Office of Naval Research Project on Methodological Aspects of Management Research, 1958.

(19) Clark, J. M., *Studies in the Economics of Overhead Costs*, Chicago: The University of Chicago Press, 1938.

(20) Cooper, W. W., "A Proposal for Extending The Theory of The Firm," *Quarterly Journal of Economics*, February, 1951.

(21) Cooper, W. W., "Historical and Alternative Costs: A Study of Some Relations Between the Economic Theory of the Firm and the Accounting Control of Operations," Unpublished Doctoral Dissertation, Columbia University, 1950.

(22) Crandall, V. J., "A Preliminary Investigation of the Generalization of Experimentally Induced Frustration in Fantasy Production," Unpublished Doctor's Dissertation, The Ohio State University, 1950, cited in J. B. Rotter (67).

(23) Cyert, R. M., W. R. Dill, and J. G. March, "The Role of Expectations in Business Decision Making," *Administrative Science Quarterly*, Vol. 3, No. 3, December, 1958.

(24) Davidson, D., P. Suppes, and S. Siegel, *Decision Making: An Experimental Approach*, Stanford: Stanford University Press, 1957.

(25) Davies, O. L. (ed.), *The Design and Analysis of Industrial Experiments*, Published for Imperical Chemical Industries Ltd., London: Oliver and Boyd, 1954.

(26) Dorfman, R., P. A. Samuelson, and R. M. Solow, *Linear Programming and Economic Analysis*, New York: McGraw-Hill Book Company, Inc., 1958.

(27) Dreze, J. H., "Individual Decision Making Under Partially Controllable Uncertainty," Unpublished Doctoral Dissertation, Columbia University, 1958.

(28) Drucker, P., *The Concept of The Corporation*, New York: John Day and Company, 1946.

(29) Edwards, W., "The Prediction of Decisions Among Bets," *Journal of Experimental Psychology*, 1955, pp. 201–214.

(30) Edwards, W., "Probability-Preference in Gambling," *American Journal of Psychology*, Vol. 66, 1954, pp. 349–364.

(31) Edwards, W., "The Theory of Decision Making," *Psychological Bulletin*, Vol. 51, 1954, pp. 380–417.

(32) Fisher, R. A., "Statistical Methods and Scientific Induction," *Journal of The Royal Statistical Society*, Series B, Vol. 17, 1955, pp. 69–78.

(33) Frank, J. D., "Individual Differences in Certain Aspects of the Level of Aspiration," *American Journal of Psychology*, Vol. 47, 1935.

(34) Heckert, J. B., *Business Budgeting and Control*, New York: The Ronald Press Company, 1946.

(35) Henrici, S. B., *Standard Costs for Manufacturing*, New York: McGraw-Hill Book Company, 1947.

(36) Hoover, H., *The Hoover Commission Report on Organization of the Executive Branch of the Government*, New York: McGraw-Hill Book Company, 1949.

(37) Hunt, J. McV. (ed.), *Personality and The Behavior Disorders*, New York: The Ronald Press Company, 2 Vols. 1954. (a) Finger, F., "Experimental Studies in the Rat;" (b) Lewin, K., Temara Dembo, L. Festinger, and Pauline S. Sears, "Level of Aspiration;" (c) Liddell, H. S., "Conditioned Reflex Method and Experimental Neurosis;" (d) Rosenzweig, S., "An Outline of Frustration Theory."

(38) Ireson, W. G., and E. L. Grant (eds.), *Handbook of Industrial Engineering and Management*, Englewood Cliffs, N. J.: Prentice-Hall, Inc., 1955.

(39) Jessor, R., "A Methodological Investigation of the Strength and Generalization of Verbal Reinforcement," Unpublished Doctoral Dissertation, The Ohio State University, 1951, cited in J. B. Rotter (67).

(40) Keller, I. W., *Management Accounting for Profit Control,* New York: McGraw-Hill Book Company, Inc., 1957.

(41) Kempthorne, O., *The Design and Analysis of Experiments,* New York: John Wiley and Sons, Inc., 1952.

(42) Klein, L. R. (ed.), *Short Term Economic Forecasting,* Vol. 17 in Studies in Income and Wealth, Conference on Research in Income and Wealth, National Bureau of Economic Research, Princeton University Press, 1955. (a) Modigliani, F., and O. H. Sauerlender, "Economic Expectations and Plans of Firms in Relation to Short-Term Forecasting;" (b) Cooper, W. W., and H. A. Simon, "Commentary."

(43) Knight, F. H., *Risk, Uncertainty, and Profit,.* London: London School of Economics and Political Science Series of Reprints of Scarce Tracts in Economics and Political Science, 1946.

(44) Kohler, E. L., *A Dictionary for Accountants,* Englewood Cliffs, N. J.: Prentice-Hall, Inc., 1956.

(45) Koopmans, T. C. (ed.), *Activity Analysis of Production and Allocation,* Cowles Commission for Research in Economics, Monograph No. 13, New York: John Wiley and Sons, Inc., 1951. (a) Dantzig, G. B., "Application of the Simplex Method to a Simplex Problem;" (b) Gale, D., H. W. Kuhn, and A. W. Tucker, "Linear Programming and the Theory of Games;" (c) Koopmans, T. C., "Analysis of Production as an Efficient Combination of Activities."

(46) Lang, T., W. B. McFarland, and M. Schiff, *Cost Accounting,* New York: The Ronald Press Company, 1953.

(47) Lanzilotti, F., "Pricing Objectives in Large Companies," *American Economic Review,* Vol. 48, No. 5, December, 1958.

(48) Lasser, J. K. (ed.), *Handbook of Cost Accounting Methods,* New York: D. Van Nostrand, Inc., 1949. (a) Sargent, C. W., "Cost Accounting as a Tool of Management."

(49) Leavitt, H. J., *Managerial Psychology: An Introduction to Individuals, Pairs, and Groups in Organization,* Chicago: The University of Chicago Press, 1958.

(50) Lincoln, J. F., *Incentive Management,* Cleveland: The Lincoln Electric Company, 1951.

(51) Lincoln, J. F., *Lincoln's Incentive System,* New York: McGraw-Hill Book Company, Inc., 1946.

(52) Luchins, A., "Mechanization in Problem Solving: The Effect of *Einstellung*," *Psychological Monograph 54*, No. 248, 1942.

(53) MacDonald, J. H., *Practical Budget Procedure*, Englewood Cliffs, N. J.: Prentice-Hall, Inc., 1939.

(54) MacGregor, D., "An Uneasy Look at Performance Appraisal," *Harvard Business Review*, Vol. 35, No. 3, May–June, 1957.

(55) Mann, H. B., *Analysis and Design of Experiments: Analysis of Variance and Analysis of Variance Designs*, New York: Dover Publications, Inc., 1949.

(56) Manne, A. S., *Scheduling of Petroleum Refinery Operations*, Cambridge: Harvard University Press, 1956.

(57) March, J. G., and H. A. Simon, *Organizations*, New York: John Wiley and Sons, 1958.

(58) Marschak, J., "Elements for a Theory of Teams," *Management Science*, Vol. 1, No. 2, January, 1955.

(59) Marschak, J., "Rational Behavior, Uncertain Prospects and Measurable Utility," *Econometrica*, Vol. 18, No. 2, April, 1950.

(60) Marshall, A., *Principles of Economics*, London: Macmillan and Company, Ltd., 1936.

(61) McFarland, W. B., "The Basic Theory of Standard Costs," *The Accounting Review*, Vol. 14, No. 2, June, 1939.

(62) Modigliani, F., and F. E. Hohn, "Planning Over Time, with Some Conclusions about the Nature of the Expectation and Planning Horizon," *Econometrica*, Vol. 23, No. 1, January, 1955.

(63) Mosteller, F., and P. Nogee, "An Experimental Measurement of Utility," *Journal of Political Economy*, Vol. 59, No. 5, October, 1951.

(63a) Radner, R., "The Application of Linear Programming to Team Decision Problems," *Management Science*, Vol. 5, No. 2, January, 1959, pp. 143–150.

(64) Rautenstrauch, W., and R. Villers, *Budgetary Control*, New York: Funk and Wagnalls Company, 1950.

(65) Robbins, H., "Some Aspects of the Sequential Design of Experiments," *Bulletin of the Mathematical Society*, Vol. 58, No. 5, September, 1952.

(66) Robnett, R. H., T. M. Hill, and J. A. Becket, *Accounting, A Management Approach*, Homewood, Illinois: Richard D. Irwin, 1954.

(67) Rotter, J. B., *Social Learning and Clinical Psychology*, Englewood Cliffs, N. J.: Prentice-Hall, Inc., 1954.

(68) Ruch, F. L., *Psychology and Life*, Chicago: Scott, Foresman and Company, 4th ed., 1953.

(69) Samuelson, P. A., *Foundations of Economic Analysis*, Cambridge: Harvard University Press, 1955.

(70) Siegel, S., "Level of Aspiration and Decision Making," *Psychological Review*, Vol. 64, No. 4, July, 1957.

(71) Simon, H. A., and H. Guetzkow, "The Impact of Certain Communication Nets upon Organization and Performance in Task-Oriented Groups," *Management Science*, Vol. 1, 1955.

(72) Simon, H. A., *Models of Man*, New York: John Wiley and Sons, Inc., 1957.

(73) Solomons, D. (ed.), *Studies in Costing*, London: Sweet and Maxwell, Ltd., 1952. (a) National Association of Accountants (formerly National Association of Cost Accountants), "A Re-Examination of Standard Costs." Reprinted from N.A.C.A. Bulletin, Vol. 29, No. 11, Section 3 (Research Series No. 11) February 1, 1948, pp. 695–727.

(74) Starbuck, W. H., "Level of Aspiration Theory and Market Behavior," Pittsburgh: Carnegie Institute of Technology, Graduate School of Industrial Administration, Behavioral Theory of Firm Project, Working Paper No. 7 (ditto), November, 1957.

(75) Stedry, A. C., "Budget Control and Cost Behavior," Pittsburgh: Carnegie Institute of Technology, Graduate School of Industrial Administration, Office of Naval Research Project on Planning and Control of Industrial Operations, ONR Research Memo. No. 60 (ditto), February, 1958.

(76) Stedry, A. C., "Computational Scheme for Optimization Under Limited Substitution of Factors," Pittsburgh: Carnegie Institute of Technology, Graduate School of Industrial Administration, Office of Naval Research Project on Planning and Control of Industrial Operations, ONR Research Memo. No. 61 (ditto), November, 1958.

(77) Stedry, A. C., "The Effect of Budgets on Individual Performances in a Problem Solving Situation — An Experiment," Pittsburgh: Carnegie Institute of Technology, Graduate School of Industrial Administration, Office of Naval Research Project on Planning and Control of Industrial Operations, ONR Research Memo. No. 63 (ditto), May 1959.

(78) Stevens, S. S. (ed.), *Handbook of Experimental Psychology*, New York: John Wiley and Sons, Inc., 1951. (a) Miller, N. E., "Learnable Drives and Rewards," pp. 435–472.

(79) Trueblood, R. M., and W. W. Cooper, "Industrial Cost Accounting," *Encyclopædia Britannica*, Chicago: William Benton, Vol. 20, pp. 126–127.

(80) Trueblood, R. M., and R. M. Cyert, *Sampling Techniques in Accounting*, Englewood Cliffs, N. J.: Prentice-Hall, Inc., 1957. (a) Cyert, R. M., and G. Meyers, "Statistical Techniques in the Control of Labor Performance," Chap. 10.

(81) Tucker, A. W., *Game Theory and Programming*, National Science Foundation Summer Mathematics Institute Notes, Stillwater: Department of Mathematics, The Oklahoma Agricultural and Mechanical College, 1955.

(82) Viteles, M. S., *Motivation and Morale in Industry*, New York: W. W. Norton and Company, Inc., 1953.

(83) Wald, A., *Statistical Decision Functions*, New York: John Wiley and Sons, Inc., 1950.

(84) Wechsler, I. R., M. Kahane, and R. Tannenbaum, "Job Satisfaction, Productivity and Morale," *Occupational Psychology*, Vol. 26, 1952, pp. 1–14.

(85) Wolfe, J. B., "Effectiveness of Token Rewards for Chimpanzees," *Comparative Psychology Monographs*, Vol. 12, No. 60, 1936.